behind the MASKS

personality

disorders

in the church

behind the
MASKS

C. MARVIN PATE, PH. D.
AND SHERYL L. PATE, M.A.

BROADMAN
& HOLMAN
PUBLISHERS

nashville, tennessee

0−8054−1843−1
Published by Broadman & Holman Publishers, Nashville, Tennessee
Editorial Team: Leonard G. Goss, John Landers
Page Design and Typesetting: TF Designs, Mount Juliet, Tennessee

Dewey Decimal Classification: 248
Subject Heading: COUNSELING

Scripture quotations are from the Holy Bible,
New International Version, copyright 1973, 1978, 1984
by International Bible Society.

Library of Congress Cataloging-in-Publication Data
Pate, C. Marvin, 1952-
    Behind the masks : personality disorders in the church / by C.
    Marvin and Sheryl Lynn Pate.
        p. cm.
    Includes bibliographical references.
    ISBN 0−8054−1843−1 (pbk.)
        1. Church work––Psychology. 2. Personality disorders––
    Religious aspects––Christianity.
    I. Pate, Sheryl Lynn, 1955– II. Title.

BV4400.P35 2000
261.8'3227––dc21   99−045168

1 2 3 4 5 04 03 02 01 00

Contents

Preface

We dedicate this study to both leadership and laity for the two-fold purpose of bringing glory to God and edification to the church. We offer a couple of observations at the outset of the book which readers should keep in mind. First, while we are not professional counselors, our twenty plus years in the pastorate have alerted us to the need for a work like this. We hope that such experience as reflected in this study contributes to a better understanding of personality disorders in the church. By divine design humans have been created to be complex, including physical, emotional and spiritual dimensions. To minister to people, therefore, requires a holistic approach, which we attempt to accomplish here through the integration of faith and psychology. Second, while the case studies presented in the following pages are true, in order to protect the privacy of others we have told their stories in composite form and without disclosing their identities.

Acknowledgments

We wish to express our sincere appreciation to a number of individuals whose invaluable assistance helped transform the idea for this book into reality. First, many thanks go to Leonard Goss and his fine staff at Broadman & Holman. Leonard's vision for, and commitment to, the project was a deep source of encouragement to us along the way, as well as that of John Landers and his skillful editing team. We also applaud the efforts and expertise of Erin Bonnell and Marty Hartley of the Moody Bible Institute, for their technical assistance in the preparation of this manuscrip. And, most especially, we wish to acknowledge the loving support of our daughter, Heather, who brings great Joy to our lives.

Grateful acknowledgment is made for permission to reprint excerpts from the following copyrighted works: *Diagnostic and Statistical Manual of Mental Disorders, Fourth Edition.* By permission of the American Psychiatric Association; ©1994. *Diagnostic and Statistical Manual of Mental Disorders, Third Edition.* By permission of the American Psychiatric Association ©1980. *Disorders of Personality, DSM III, Axis II* by Theodore Million. By permission of John Wiley and Sons Copyright ©1981 by Theodore Million. *The New Personality Self-Portrait* by John M. Oldham and Lois B. Morris. By permission of Bantam Books Copyright ©1995 by John M. Oldham and Lois B. Morris. *Cognitive Therapy of Personality Disorders* by Aaron T. Beck, Arthur Freeman and Associates. *The DSM-IV Personality Disorders* by W. John Livesley, ed. By permission of The Guilford Press Copyright ©1995 by John Livesley, ed. *Doomsday Delusions* by Calvin B. Haines and C. Marvin Pate. By permission of InterVarsity Press Copyright ©1995 by Calvin B. Haines and C. Marvin Pate.

C. Marvin and Sheryl L. Pate

◆ Introduction ◆

The Eclipse and Reemergence of the Soul

We have all been mesmerized by the sight of a solar eclipse, the brilliance of the sun becoming gradually blocked from view by the moon as it appears to move across the face of the sun, obliterating its light. In this chapter, we will discuss the eclipse of a soul and its restoration to wholeness in the context of personality types and personality disorders. Using the analogy of a solar eclipse, the moon is to the sun as personality disorders are to personality types. Allow us to explain.

Representing the sun in our analogy, every person is created in the image of God and, through the combination of nature and nurture, possesses a personality type with a unique strength through which the light of God can shine. There are those, however, who are only a "shadow" of who they have been created to be. Over time, a personality disorder in which a negative personality trait has become dominant, the moon in this analogy, gradually eclipses the light, blocking out the strength of an individual's personality type more and more until potentially it can entirely disappear from view.

The good news is that the eclipse of a soul does not have to be a permanent condition. Just as in a solar eclipse, the moon appears to eventually move across the sun, revealing more and more of its light, the transforming power of the Holy Spirit can once again reveal the strength of an individual's personality style, restoring the individual to healthy, normal functioning in the world.

John: "Lonesome Dove"

Meet John, a man in his midforties, who has an earned doctorate, is a professor, a minister, an author, a happily married man, and a loving father. Few who knew John forty years ago would have dreamed he would achieve this much. John's alcoholic father brought shame to the young teenager. John developed poor self-esteem from seeing his father drunk in public, from suffering constant tension in his home, and from living in the poverty his father's alcoholism imposed on his family. He had little self-confidence, developed few close friends, and avoided social functions. Others' less-than-positive comments about him made things worse.

John developed the avoidant personality disorder that understandably results when a child is repeatedly exposed to core experiences that shame him or her. Suffering from poor self-esteem, such people, through no fault of their own, have become ashamed of themselves, thereby rendering them socially inept. What made the difference for John? Simply put, the joy of the Holy Spirit eventually overcame the eclipse of his soul, enabling the sun of his God-given personality to shine through. Today, although John still has to deal with his social inhibitions, he is no longer shame-based. Rather, the Spirit of Christ has empowered him to accomplish significant goals, not the least of which is to relate well to people, both privately and publicly.

Drawing on the three phases of an eclipse as an outline, this Introduction will overview the relationship between personality styles and personality disorders: phase one—the dawning of personality styles; phase two—the eclipse of personality strengths by personality disorders; phase three—the reemergence of the personality strengths by the power of the Spirit.

First Phase: The Dawning of Personality

Personality is universal and represented in every individual by a unique constellation of traits or characteristics which remain surprisingly consistent over time despite life experiences. Oldham and Morris state, "Your personality style is your organizing principle. It propels you on your life path. It represents the orderly arrangement of all your attributes, thoughts, feelings, attitudes, behaviors, and coping mechanisms. It is the distinctive pattern of your psychological functioning—the way you think, feel, and behave—that makes you *definitely* you."[1] This unique blending of characteristics is often called the individual's personality type or personality style and reflects orderly human functioning. This includes the flexibility to deal with everyday problems, to respond appropriately to varied situations, and to adapt in dealing with obstacles in life.[2]

The Study of Personality

The study of personality development and traits is most fascinating. Hippocrates, in the fifth century B.C., was the first to postulate four temperament types (sanguine = enthusiastic; melancholic = sad; choleric = aggressive; phlegmatic = apathetic). Rooted in his work, Braund and Voges, who espouse the DISC system of personality types, first articulated by William Marston (Dominant, Influencing, Steadiness, Compliance), and Oldham and Morris who speak of some seventeen personality styles based on the American Psychiatric Association's *Diagnostic and Statistical Manual III*, reflect the continuing interest in our society regarding personality. In this work, we will focus on what we believe are the eight essential personality styles and their respective strengths (based on DSM-IV, to which we will later refer). They are as follows:

Personality Portrait and Strength

"The Sentinel"	Ever-Ready
"The Maverick"	Daring
"The Rebel"	Energetic
"The Entertainer"	Fun Loving
"The Star"	Magnetic
"The Lonesome Dove"	Unassuming
"The Follower"	Faithful
"The Achiever"	Persevering

Is a personality type determined by nature or nurture? Undoubtedly by both. The genetic makeup of the various personalities is receiving increased emphasis these days. Thus, in their April 1998 article in *Life*, Colt and Hollister state, "In one of the most bitter scientific controversies of the 20th century—the battle over nature and nurture—a wealth of new research has tipped the scales overwhelmingly toward nature. Studies of twins and advances in molecular biology have uncovered a more significant genetic component to personality than was previously known."[3] James Dobson, a leading family psychologist, states in his book *Parenting Isn't for Cowards*, "It is my supposition that these temperaments are prepackaged before birth and do not have to be cultivated or encouraged."[4]

Ordinary experience attests the genetic basis of personality styles, for many parents remark that each of their children behaved differently from birth. One university psychologist comments, "Every parent of one child is an environmentalist, and every parent of more than one becomes a geneticist."[5] The Scriptures confirm the reality that heredity is a significant component of personality types in that they are by divine design:

> "For you created my inmost being;
>   you knit me together in my mother's womb.
> I praise you because I am fearfully and wonderfully made;
>   your works are wonderful,
> I know that full well."
>   (Ps. 139:13–14).

Even so, nurture and environment undeniably also play a role in the development of personality traits. Effective parenting helps to create the proper setting for children to grow into the people God has created them to be. This may well be what Proverbs 22:6 means:

> "Train a child in the way he should go,
> and when he is old he will not turn from it."

This verse has traditionally been understood to mean that parents should raise children up with moral teaching (which is certainly important), but it may also indicate that parents are to train children in harmony with their natural, God-given bent ("the *way* he should *naturally* go"). According to Voges and Braund this verse "may refer to creating a healthy and understanding environment in which the child can mature in accordance with his individual personality profile, or temperament."[6] We believe that Scripture and experience recognize both heredity and environment as components of personality types.

Second Phase: Personality Disorders as the Eclipse of the Personality Strength

Personality traits perform effectively in a healthy individual with a personality type or style. They function in unhealthy and maladaptive ways in personality disorders. There is, in fact, a continuum along which these operate, ranging from healthy to unhealthy.

While we all are imperfect and possess human "eccentricities," those with personality disorders consistently respond to life in maladaptive ways. They develop long-term, inflexible, repetitious patterns of behavior that result in subjective distress and/or difficulties in interpersonal relationships.[7] What happens, for example, if the star has a dominant characteristic of selfishness that consistently overshadows the strength of a magnetic personality? The individual is then said to be narcissistic. If the follower allows himself or herself to be controlled by others, the individual is said to have a dependent personality disorder. If mavericks go too far down their own paths, they manifest antisocial behaviors. While these individuals are not suffering from a serious psychiatric disorder, and thus are capable of functioning in society, having a personality disorder is a troubled way of being in the world, which represents an extreme of normal human patterns. The difference is often only one of degree and thus personality disorders represent exaggerations of personality types.[8]

Each of the eight personality types has a corresponding personality disorder. Disorder results when one particular characteristic comes to dominate an individual's life. We will address each of these eight personality disorders and explain how they affect the persons with these conditions and how they disrupt the lives of others who live with them. This chart shows the weakness that corresponds to each personality disorder:

Personality Disorder and Dominant Characteristic

Obsessive-Compulsive	Perfectionistic
Histrionic	Pleasure
Dependent	Controlled
Narcissistic	Selfish
Avoidant	Intimidated
Paranoid	Fear
Antisocial	Hostility
Borderline	Out of control

The *Diagnostic and Statistical Manual* (DSM-III), which offered a new system of diagnostic categories for personality disorders in 1980, predecessor of DSM-III-R (1983) and DSM-IV (1994), defines personality disorders as follows:

> It is only when personality traits are inflexible and maladaptive and cause either significant impairment in social or occupational functioning or subjective distress that they constitute personality disorders. The manifestations of personality disorders are generally recognizable by adolescence or earlier and continue through most of adult life, though they often become less obvious in middle or old age ... the diagnosis of a "personality disorder" should be made only when the characteristic features are typical of the individual's long-term functioning and are not limited to discrete episodes of illness.[9]

Individuals with personality disorders display a distorted way of living, managing their affairs and relationships,[10] having persistent, maladaptive ways of perceiving, thinking, and relating to the world around them. They do not see themselves as the major contributing cause to their own difficulties.[11] However, they often leave a trail of disturbed interpersonal relationships with behavior that is persistent and long-term in nature, coloring each new situation they meet. The effect of a personality disorder in a person's life can often graphically be seen by its effect on others, with patterns of behavior highly resistant to change. They often do not understand why things don't work out or the effect their actions have on others.[12]

The behavioral patterns of personality disorders were not clearly described until publication of the American Psychiatric Association's first *Diagnostic and Statistical Manual* (DSM-1) in 1952. Prior to that time, they were simply considered to be "disorders of character" found in otherwise normal people. Over the last fifteen years scientific understanding regarding personality disorders has exploded as it has developed into an active field of clinical research. This is largely due to the groundbreaking effort of the American Psychiatric Association's DSM-III (1980), which classified personality disorders and provided explicit diagnostic criteria for each condition. Further scientifically grounded data provided the basis for DSM III-R (1983) and DSM-IV (1994).

While scientific research has resulted in tremendous growth in knowledge regarding personality types and personality disorders in the past two decades, much is still to be learned and clarified in this field of study. For example, the criteria for personality disorders is not seen to be as clearly defined as other diagnostic criteria. In this book, as in Oldham and Morris, we will view personality traits on a continuum ranging from healthy, normal functioning (personality types) to extreme, maladaptive functioning (personality disorders). The study of personality is based on traits, with personality type and personality disorder being defined by traits rather than by behavior, although behavior is an indicator of the presence of characteristics associated with specific personality types and personality disorders. For the purpose of our study, we will address eight personality types and personality disorders, and while individuals can show characteristics of more than one personality type or personality disorder, often one is more dominant than another.

Because personality traits can be viewed on a continuum, one must keep in mind that the characteristics associated with personality disorders can be found on a smaller scale in many normal individuals. However, the long-term, exaggerated nature of personality traits causing subjective distress and/or affecting the individual's interpersonal relationships provides the basis for defining a personality disorder.

The question of a biological origin of personality disorders is being researched. Some theorists believe there is a hereditary or constitutional predisposition toward personality disorders, while others emphasize early life experiences and learned habit patterns.[13] Although some research suggests that genetic factors may be involved in the development of some personality disorders, such as the paranoid personality and the borderline personality, a constitutional basis is largely hypothetical with the possible exception of the antisocial personality. Millon states, "Individuals with similar biological potentials emerge with different personality patterns depending on their environmental experiences. These patterns unfold as new maturations interweave with new environmental encounters. In time, learned attitudes and behaviors stabilize into a distinctive hierarchy of traits that remain relatively consistent through the ever-changing stream of experience."[14] Oldham and Morris summarize the impact of our life experiences as follows: "Life shapes what will become of our genetic possibilities—but our inborn nature also affects what will happen to us."[15]

What does this all mean for the church? When a person's life is thrown off balance by loss of a job, a divorce, death of a spouse, or other crises, a window of opportunity often presents itself for the church to minister to the individual, for during such times people with personality disorders often become aware that they have a problem. Openness to an encounter with God at that critical juncture can effect no less than a dramatic, permanent life transformation. In these instances, long-standing personality patterns and behaviors in need of alteration can be addressed as people encounter the love of the risen Jesus and become new persons in Christ. Indeed, an individual's personality can be entirely reordered.[16] This is truly good news!

The reality, however, in many churches today is that "formal religious influences have generally left these underlying formations of personality untouched."[17] In fact, for people with personality disorders "religious behavior has taken the form of the personality disorder more often than religious experience has wrought a deep change in the pattern of this disorder. In short, the person's basic way of life continues as it was."[18] Sadly, Oates notes that behaviors associated with personality disorders are seen to be "worthy models to be copied, and as necessary for getting somewhere in our competitive and aggressive American culture."[19] Churches adopting a corporate model for growth (competition to be bigger) "tend to glorify some of the personality disorders, such as the aggressive antisocial way of life, the grandiose paranoid way of life and the self-absorbed narcissistic way of life. At the same time, they tend to exploit persons laboring under the weight of other personality disorders such as the dependent, the histrionic . . . and compulsive ways of life."[20] Our society values an outgoing, vivacious personality as opposed to an introverted, shy personality. Are our churches any different? All too often, the gregarious, attractive, and active personalities are held up as models of spirituality in order to "win the lost."

Richard's Story

A pastor of a growing church was delighted to welcome into his congregation a new couple—Susan and Richard. Richard, a former administrator of a Christian school, commanded attention with his charisma and self-assured demeanor. Susan, in contrast, was quiet and reserved and preferred not to be in the limelight. Richard quickly acquired center stage in the church, filling a vacancy as Christian Education Director. Not long after that, several teachers in the various departments resigned their positions. Their reasons for doing so? Richard was too demanding of their time and energy; moreover, he displayed an inflexible attitude in his dealings with others, bullying them into doing things his way. About the same time, Richard started a small business with his cousin. Suddenly advertisements promoting their business began cropping up in the church (bulletin boards, bulletins, etc.), something without precedent in that congregation. Interestingly enough, Richard hired a number of the church's members, none of whom remained with the company long. One of them observed, "The only one making any profit in the business was Richard."

While all of this was going on, Richard began to speak of alienation from his sister. Apparently she took exception to his decision to transfer all of their father's money into his own account after Richard's father, recently widowed, had come to live with Richard and Susan. When his father died, not long thereafter, Richard's company doubled in size. His sister accused him of taking more than his share of their father's inheritance. To make a long story short, Richard's aggressive actions, which placed him front and center stage in the church, along with telling a number of lies that implicated members of the congregation, prompted the pastor and elders to confront him. Rather than humbling himself and repenting, he and his adoring wife stormed out of the church, never to return. Later, the pastor learned that Richard had done similar things in another church, also causing his expulsion.

The case study just rehearsed is a rather typical story of what happens when a person suffering from narcissistic personality disorder is permitted to quickly advance in a church's ministry. The core of Richard's problem was egotism, a problem born out of a less-than-affirming relationship with his mother. The results were sad indeed. Every area of Richard's life—church, work, family—were adversely affected. Had that pastor known the true nature of the situation, he surely would not have given Richard full run of the church.

What happens when those in authority in the church are not aware of the ramifications personality disorders can have on the health of their congregation? Many a church leader has been used by congregational members suffering from a personality disorder. These individuals feel no need to be exposed to the effect their behavior has on others and seem mystified by the misery experienced by those with whom they are intimately related. Sometimes these individuals simply move from church to church, never understanding or taking responsibility for the chaos and broken relationships their behavior has left behind.

While the story of Richard focuses on church members, the problem of personality disorders in the church is by no means limited to those sitting in the pews. For example, the paranoid or antisocial pastor who advocates harsh or legalistic religious dogmatism, using it to punish parishioners from the pulpit, is engaged in a form of verbal abuse, which itself can produce avoidant, compulsive or antisocial personality disorders in the congregation[21] or, one might add, wreak havoc on those already predisposed to such conditions.

Of course, the church exists in a cultural framework. The Christian community rightly points to the "shallowness and defectiveness of our cultural values, beliefs, and expectations; and parent-child relationships" as contributing to the creation of personality disorders, which are maladaptive ways of coping with life's difficulties and relating to others.[22] Individuals such as Millon see the antecedent cause of personality disorders to be learned coping strategies.[23] If an individual has grown up in a family in which other members have personality disorders (for example, distrust of strangers), an individual may identify with these defective adjustments because no other model has been provided.[24] Those with personality disorders tend to gravitate toward others with complementary personality disorders, creating a cluster of personality disorders within a family, an organization, or a church.

Third Phase: The Reemergence of Personality Strengths

Can individuals with a personality disorder truly be restored to wholeness in which the strength of their personality type once again shines through? Absolutely. Individual lives have been transformed by the power of the Holy Spirit. An integral part of the journey back to wholeness involves the ongoing support of a Christian community.

As believers, how can we genuinely minister to those afflicted with personality disorders? First, the church must become aware of these conditions. We must educate ourselves, as well as those possessing the behavioral characteristics of personality disorders, and be honest in self-examination regarding the presence of these distorted perspectives on life. As churches reflect their culture, they must be willing to examine whether they are unwittingly holding up a personality disorder as a model of spirituality, for example, the paranoid, histrionic, obsessive-compulsive, or dependent types.

Second, the church must reappraise its view of ministry to those suffering from personality disorders in order to help them achieve psychological health and then to minister to one another and to a hurting world. Simply put, the church's challenge is to tailor its responses to the respective personality deficiencies. For example, the fear of the paranoid will need to be allayed; the borderline personality will require an unconditionally loving environment in which to formulate their identity; the obsessive-compulsive will be set free by an emphasis on grace; and the dependent will soar to independence when they are helped to realize their rightful authority in Christ. And, somewhere along the line, all of those demonstrating personality disorders should be encouraged to seek professional counseling.

Third, the church should strive to accept all personality types, with their respective strengths and weaknesses. A church that is inclusive in perspective will welcome, for example, the entertainer's fun-loving heart, the humility of the lonesome dove, and the conscientiousness of the achiever. And when a particular trait becomes dominant, overshadowing the strength and becoming a detriment, the church will also point those individuals to the respective fruit of the Spirit needed to bring them back into balance and harmonious relationships.

The reemergence of personality strengths generally occurs over time in the life of an individual with a personality disorder as the fruit of the Spirit provides the missing ingredient in the person's life. It is not an easy process or a "quick fix," but as persons come to grapple with their need and the power of the Holy Spirit to restore them to wholeness, in the environment of a nurturing and discerning Christian community, they can truly become the persons they were meant to be.

In the chapters which follow, we will examine each of the personality types and personality disorders and discuss the implications for those with such aberrant behavior as well as those who are in a relationship with the affected persons. Moreover, to help explain the personality disorders, we will identify feelings generated in those encountering an individual with a personality disorder, supply biblical examples which illustrate each of the conditions, and show how the fruit of the Spirit provides the ultimate solution to the root problems plaguing these people. Finally, we will discuss the healthy personality, of which Jesus is the perfect example, a model of psychological health. The chart on the following page offers a road map to the contents of this book:

Personality Portrait and Strength	Personality Disorder and Dominant Characteristic	Feelings Generated In Others	Biblical Example	Fruit
The Achiever— Persevering	Obsessive-Compulsive— Perfectionistic	Controlled, frustrated, manipulated, anxious	Paul	Longsuffering
The Entertainer— Fun Loving	Histrionic— Pleasure	Flattered, entertained, impressed, "drawn to," betrayed	Mark	Faithfulness
The Follower— Faithful	Dependent— Controlled	Sympathetic, frustrated, helpless	Mary Magdalene	Meekness (power under control)
The Star— Magnetic	Narcissistic— Selfishness	Threatened, inferior, manipulated	Woman at the well	Goodness
The Lonesome Dove— Unassuming	Avoidant— Intimidated	Uncomfortable, confused, guilty	Moses	Joy
The Sentinel— Ever-ready	Paranoid— Fear	Fear, anxiety, dislike, suspicion	Herod the Great	Peace
The Maverick— Daring	Antisocial — Hostility	Anxious, manipulated, controlled, defensive, envious	Cain	Gentleness
The Rebel— Energetic	Borderline— Out of control	Confused, attacked, intimidated	Samson	Self-control

◆ One ◆

The Achiever and Obsessive-Compulsive Personality Disorder

Seize the day! is an apt phrase representing the achiever's approach to life. These people are task-oriented and thrive on challenge. They are the "doers" of this world. Through dedication and commitment to their goals, they can overcome great obstacles. Being aware that we are given only a limited number of days on this earth, they make the most of each moment to develop and use the gifts and talents God has given them.

A quick browse through the psychology, self-help, or biography section in any bookstore will yield a multitude of motivational books. These books often contain stories of individuals who, though enduring great hardships, persevered and accomplished great things. These books can inspire, encourage, and motivate us to believe in our God-given dreams, as these achievers have done, and "go for it"!

Achievers share at least one commonality—perseverance in the pursuit of their goals. Without this trait their dreams would not become realities because they know that achievement happens only through hard work and over time. They commit themselves to the long haul. We all want achievers on our team when there is a job to be done, for we know they will persevere until the task is complete. They are a great asset to any church or community with the take-charge stance and positive mental attitude characteristic of these individuals.

Our society has, of course, been built on this work ethic, and in cultures such as ours the achiever thrives. At its best, this type of environment produces individuals who leave great legacies as they push the frontiers of medicine, education, and music. Their persistence and determination yield incredible results. These people are tenacious to the max, believing in and using their God-given abilities as they seek to make a difference in this world.

Achievers, possessing the strength of endurance, fulfill their life purpose in a healthy, functional way. As we have seen, personality traits can operate on a continuum, from healthy to unhealthy ways of believing and behaving. What happens when individuals achieve, not out of a sense of gratitude for the gifts that God has given them and a desire to make the world a better place, but out of a shame-based sense of desperation to control themselves and others, endeavoring to prove their worth, time and time again? This is a portrait of individuals whose strength—their conscientious, persevering approach to life—is dominated and overshadowed by fear and shame to the extent the strength is eclipsed, with its extreme nature actually becoming a liability rather than a strength. This distortion of the strength of the achiever is characteristic of an individual with a personality disorder.

The Achiever Versus
Obsessive-Compulsive Personality Disorder

The difference between the personality portrait of the achiever, whose primary strength is perseverance, and an individual possessing obsessive-compulsive personality disorder, like that of all the other personality disorders, is a matter of degree and the consequences of the individual's behavior.[1] While everyone experiences self-doubt, and many perhaps have tried to achieve a goal to get the approval of a parent or a teacher, all do not experience obsessive-compulsive personality disorder. Rather, consistent, extreme behaviors such as perfectionism to the point of not being able to function adequately and inflexibility in dealing with life, needing absolute control over oneself and others, clue one in to the existence of obsessive-compulsive personality disorder. These desperately unhappy individuals cannot relate to themselves or others in healthy ways.

Society, as well as the church, can unwittingly reinforce the behaviors associated with personality disorders. In *We Are Driven*, Hemfelt, Minirth, and Meier note the tendency of society to reward unhealthy, compulsive, and perfectionistic tendencies with its overemphasis on individualism and competition. They refer to them as "the compulsions America applauds."[2] This drivenness produces negative consequences physically, emotionally, and spiritually. They define *drivenness* as "an insatiable drive to do more and be more. It's a drive that may be masked by charitable and positive motives, but in reality originates in deep, perhaps even unconscious, feelings of inadequacy and shame."[3]

Hemfelt, Minirth, and Meier use the terms *drivenness, compulsivity*, and *applauded addictions* interchangeably to refer to a type of society-sanctioned personality style and lifestyle characterized by "performance and perfection pressures" that they say have reached epidemic proportions. This is based on the faulty belief that one's worth depends on achievement. They root this inability to love and value oneself apart from achievement in spiritual alienation where one is unable to accept God's unconditional love.[4]

Susan's Story

"I don't know how to make things better," Susan says. "I feel afraid and nervous all the time. I try so hard, but I can't seem to get it right."

It is difficult to believe this is the same woman who presents an impeccable, professional image day after day in the office and serves as a dedicated leader in her church where she coordinates outreach ministries.

Her inner life has been falling apart for some time now, and she has chosen to seek the help of her pastor because of feelings of depression and anxiety. Something is going wrong on her way to the "American dream." On the job she struggles to maintain her productivity, yet she seems to get lost in the details of a project, unable to see tasks in perspective. She spends almost all her waking hours at her office, often arriving by 6:30 A.M. and staying well into the night. Her secretary frequently becomes frustrated by Susan's unrealistic and unreasonable expectations of her. Susan resents her secretary taking even a few moments for a coffee break, asserting that the woman is not dedicated enough to her job. She complains that others frequently waste time on the job socializing and discussing personal matters.

Her superiors, while applauding her dedication, cite her lack of interpersonal skills (not socializing with colleagues or gaining rapport with clients) as preventing her from achieving greater status in the company. Susan is angered by their assertions, claiming that it is her dedication to the company which has put it "on the map," and she is desperately angry that others who "play ball" get promoted, leaving her behind. She states that promotion in the business depends on having a charismatic personality rather than on hard work and responsible behavior. She sees herself as sacrificing her personal life for the good of the company and says she feels unappreciated.

During the few waking hours in which Susan is not at work, she is involved in leading a number of activities at church. Those with whom she has served on committees have frequently resigned from their positions, complaining to the pastor that Susan has totally unrealistic, perfectionistic expectations of what is to be done. In turn, Susan has bitterly denounced others' lack of dedication and states that she is left with all the responsibility for things getting done right. She says she feels overburdened and overwhelmed by all her work and church responsibilities.

Susan is suffering from obsessive-compulsive personality disorder. As Oldham and Morris state, "Individuals suffering from the disorder are so exceedingly conscientious that they can no longer adapt to the demands of reality or meet their personal and professional goals, and to others they may seem exasperating, even impossible, to deal with."[5] They may appear to be "drowning in minutiae" as they are consumed by details.[6]

For these people "control, responsibility, and systematization" dominate to such an extent, that they are unable to engage in spontaneity and playfulness without great anxiety. The two key words which summarize their lives are "control" and "should."[7] They view themselves as responsible and strive to be seen as competent, while frequently viewing others as irresponsible, self-indulgent, and lazy. They believe that their way is the best and only way to complete any task effectively, that details are exceedingly important, and that people should endeavor to try harder.[8] Their whole life centers around trying to get it "right," experiencing great anxiety when their perception of control is threatened. Their view of rules involves rigidity and inflexibility, and they are enraged when another person is seen to have broken "the rules" without punishment because of their paradoxical subconscious desires to rebel and yet to get the approval of others through obedience.[9] Driven by perfectionism, they are quick to criticize and try to control their own and others' behavior in the name of "striving for excellence."

Criteria for Obsessive-Compulsive Personality Disorder

The DSM-IV lists the following criteria for obsessive-compulsive personality disorder:

A pervasive pattern of preoccupation with orderliness, perfectionism, and mental and interpersonal control, at the expense of flexibility, openness, and efficiency, beginning by early adulthood and present in a variety of contexts, as indicated by four (or more) of the following:

1. is preoccupied with details, rules, lists, order, organization, or schedules to the extent that the major point of the activity is lost
2. shows perfectionism that interferes with task completion (e.g., is unable to complete a project because his or her own overly strict standards are not met)
3. is excessively devoted to work and productivity to the exclusion of leisure activities and friendships (not accounted for by obvious economic necessity)
4. is overconscientious, scrupulous, and inflexible about matters of morality, ethics, or values (not accounted for by cultural or religious identification)
5. is unable to discard worn-out or worthless objects even when they have no sentimental value
6. is reluctant to delegate tasks or to work with others unless they submit to exactly his or her way of doing things
7. adopts a miserly spending style toward both self and others; money is viewed as something to be hoarded for future catastrophes
8. shows rigidity and stubbornness[10]

At their core, those with this personality disorder chafe against the rigid controls on their life, desperately struggling to control their anxiety by maintaining control over themselves and others. Kennedy and Charles are correct when they state that obsessive-compulsive individuals possess a great deal of masked anger.[11] In fact, their entire lives are about controlling the rage that subconsciously boils inside them. They are terrified of losing control and destroying themselves or others or of being rejected and abandoned for being found out as incompetent and "worthless." While obsessive-compulsive individuals are often critical, and even punishing of others for not being perfect, they often inflict the greatest punishment on themselves, mercilessly inflicting psychological pain for the smallest of "infractions." Obsessive-compulsives can be aptly described as "living machines,"[12] as they suppress their emotions and focus on productivity as the measure of human worth.

The behavior of an obsessive-compulsive individual may be mystifying and absurd to an onlooker because it may appear to defy logic. While obsessive-compulsive people highly value productivity and competence, their behavior can often be self-defeating and even self-destructive as their perfectionism and craving for control prevent them from, rather than lead them to, accomplishing their tasks. In fact, looking for the perfect way to complete a task and avoid making mistakes may take such precedence in their minds and become so time-consuming that completing the task becomes lost and the means becomes all encompassing. "These individuals make a virtue of justifying the means to achieve the end to such an extent that the means becomes an end in itself. To them, 'orderliness is godliness.' "[13]

Belief System of Individuals with Obsessive-Compulsive Personality Disorder

The following are typical beliefs held by those with obsessive-compulsive personality disorder:

1. I am fully responsible for myself and others.
2. I have to depend on myself to see that things get done.
3. Others tend to be too casual, often irresponsible, self-indulgent, or incompetent.
4. It is important to do a perfect job on everything.
5. I need order, systems, and rules in order to get the job done properly.
6. If I don't have systems, everything will fall apart.
7. Any flaw or defect of performance may lead to a catastrophe.
8. It is necessary to stick to the highest standards at all times, or things will fall apart.
9. I need to be in complete control of my emotions.
10. People should do things my way.
11. If I don't perform at the highest level, I will fail.
12. Flaws, defects, or mistakes are intolerable.
13. Details are extremely important.
14. My way of doing things is generally the best way.[14]

Feelings Experienced by Others

As we have seen, feelings experienced by others are important in detecting the existence of a personality disorder. What does one feel when in the presence of an individual with obsessive-compulsive personality disorder? Feelings of being controlled, frustrated, manipulated, or anxious are typical. Exasperation at the inflexibility of these individuals is often experienced and frustration at the seemingly superior, "self righteous" attitude with which they approach others is also common. Their excessive need for control leaves others feeling manipulated and used. Excluded from the decision-making process, others feel that they are simply part of an obsessive-compulsive's agenda and the means to an end of accomplishing a task which the obsessive-compulsive has deemed important.

Cloud and Townsend, in *Safe People,* comment that others may feel "disconnected" (as these people resist true intimacy); "one down" (in an inferior position); "weaker than one really is" (vulnerable); "dependent on the 'strong one' " (dependent); experiencing "anger and hostility at the 'together' one" (as perfectionists tend to present themselves as "together" and in control); or "feeling the need to compete to reverse the role (trapped in a weaker position and attempting to fight it)."[15]

Their statements concerning perfectionists aptly reflect the experience of people dealing with an individual with obsessive-compulsive personality disorder. As they state, "Perfectionists demand that their friends be perfect.... Generally perfectionists opt for isolation rather than to be exposed in their failings. It is sadly ironic that perfectionists shun the very safety that could heal them."[16]

It is almost impossible for those not possessing obsessive-compulsive personality disorder to understand the depth of suffering of these individuals, for they frequently do not appear to be suffering at all. In fact, they often seem oblivious to their own part in interpersonal difficulties, instead blaming others, for example, for "not trying hard enough." They are unwilling or unable to change their own attitudes and behaviors. While a person with dependent personality disorder may come across as pathetic and needy, thus eliciting sympathy and understanding, obsessive-compulsives do not elicit such a response with their aloof sense of correctness and critical, perfectionistic tendencies.

While obsessive-compulsives do not appear to have any tolerance for human imperfections and failings, terror exists behind their facade of control and perfection. These desperately hurting individuals crave being accepted for who they are, imperfections and all. They often feel a great sense of isolation from others, unknowingly self-imposed, as they commonly feel alternately superior (when they have performed well according to their standards) and inferior to others (when having fallen short of their own or others' expectations). The experience of human emotion, necessary for creating and maintaining healthy interpersonal relationships, is threatening to obsessive-compulsives, and they commonly "shut down" emotions to avoid overwhelming anxiety.

Factors in the Development of Obsessive-Compulsive Personality Disorder: Nature Versus Nurture

What causes an individual to develop obsessive-compulsive personality disorder? While much is still to be learned about the development of personality disorders, the debate over nature versus nurture continues. Some believe children may be born with a predisposition to develop obsessive-compulsive personality disorder, while others emphasize the role which one's environment plays in the development of personality disorders. The obsessive-compulsive experiences the world as a threatening place and believes that only "getting it right" can ensure safety.

Home Environment

What experiences in a person's past could create and reinforce such beliefs? Sullivan viewed low self-esteem as a primary problem caused by a home environment in which much anger is hidden behind a superficial facade of love and niceness.[17] This would account for a great deal of ambivalence and confusion experienced by a child and thus the need to create a sense of order and gain control over one's life. Angyal also cited the low self-esteem of those with obsessive-compulsive personality disorder and believed it had its basis in "inconsistent, often contradictory behavior of the parents." Either the actions and feelings appeared to be contradictory to their words, or else they appeared to behave in "very erratic, seemingly irrational ways," for example, affectionate then cold. Confusion was created in the child by the parents' contradictory demands or "failure to practice what they preach."[18] Guidano and Liotti have found that those with obsessive-compulsive personality disorder "usually grow up in a home in which they are given very mixed, contradictory messages from at least one of their parents."[19] This places children in a double bind, and they cannot "win" regardless of their behavior. For example, if a parent espouses traditional moral values and communicates the expectations for a child that these standards of behavior are expected and yet seeks the company of those whose behavior contradicts those standards, the child experiences great confusion. Also, if a parent's behavior is inconsistent, contradictory, or manipulative (frequently to control others), a child can develop the characteristics associated with obsessive-compulsive personality disorder in order to experience some control over his or her world. In these cases, a child's psyche is literally torn apart by the contradictory messages, leaving a chasm at the core of the individual's being, which the individual tries to fill with "magical" rituals intended to provide safety.

Millon and Everly attribute development of obsessive-compulsive personality disorder to overcontrolling parents.[20] The child is punished for displaying autonomy and thus does not form a separate identity. Either subtly manipulative or overtly dominant, controlling parents create a dysfunctional relationship with their children in which the children remain unhealthily "enmeshed" with them and experience great distress when not in the presence of their "protector" parents. Through the experience of being overcontrolled, these children crave control in order to feel safe. These children do not form healthy, necessary emotional boundaries between themselves and others. Denying a child's sense of autonomy (setting appropriate limits but acknowledging the right of the child to have differing beliefs and feelings) can lead to the individual's becoming an adult who cannot say no to others when they violate emotional or physical boundaries.[21]

The experience of a chaotic home can also predispose a child to develop an elaborate schema of rules and order in an effort to achieve a sense of security and stability. This can occur in homes where there is obvious neglect or violence. However, a more subtle form of chaos can also take place. In a home where a parent consistently makes minor events into catastrophes and where drama is commonplace, imagined evils looming large and threatening to destroy the family, the child can develop great insecurities, with obsessions and compulsions being a natural outcome. For example, a parent may become a "prayer chain junkie" of sorts, with children constantly hearing of church members, their friends and relatives who suffer tragedies, thus predisposing them to believe that life is full of only heartache and misery.

In addition, growing up in a family in which one (or both) of the parents have never grown up emotionally can contribute to the development of obsessive-compulsive personality disorder in a child. The child and parent roles are switched, and the child is expected to meet the needs of the parent and function as an adult. Because a child lacks the maturity and experiences necessary to take on the responsibilities of adulthood, and yet is expected to do so, the child may assume that elaborate rules and order must be necessary to preserve safety in the environment. These excessive rules, though inappropriate, can persist, well beyond the time they were seen as being needed for survival. Deprived of an adult role model, instead of the reversal of roles, the child can become "stuck" emotionally. Then, even after becoming an adult, the obsessive-compulsive tries to control the world with these same perceptions of a child who is trying to fend off a hostile world.

Role of the Church

Unfortunately, not only society's excessive focus on achievement and worth through performance but also parental "mixed messages," manipulation, or overcontrolling of children can foster the development of obsessive-compulsive personality disorder. The church itself can also unwittingly contribute to the existence of this personality disorder. Churches in which shame and guilt are used to control people or in which people are expected to abdicate all control of their lives to a tyrannical yet perhaps "dictator" God can contribute to the development of characteristics associated with obsessive-compulsive personality disorder among their members. If individuals are shame-based, have little trust in their abilities to control "unwanted" impulses, and feel as if they can be rejected at any time by God, an almost intolerable situation results. Rules are needed to exert control over oneself in order not to transgress, and yet paradoxically the individual seeks to "act out" in the desperate hope that perhaps there is, after all, a God who loves us just the way we are.

For those experiencing obsessive-compulsive personality disorder, only some form of abuse can account for the depth of internal suffering experienced by these wounded souls, the inappropriate use of power by others to control them wreaking havoc in their lives. Having been abused, they not only mistrust their own competency to handle life but lack confidence in the trustworthiness of others as well. They appear to be missing something at the core of their beings, which is crucial for becoming a healthy, well-adjusted person; they were most likely deprived of a sense of security, safety, and trust in childhood.

Their aversion to experiencing genuine human emotion, and thus their "mechanistic" approach to life, is a defense tactic. It protects them from the awareness that they have been mistreated, for if they acknowledged the emotional abuse perpetrated on them as vulnerable children, and the reality that they had no control over the situation, subconsciously they fear that the ensuing rage could engulf and destroy themselves and others. Thus, this knowledge is suppressed, and they continue to suffer what they believe is the "lesser of two evils."

Hope and Help

Is there hope for an individual suffering from obsessive-compulsive personality disorder? Absolutely! Let's look at the life of a biblical character who personifies what can happen when an individual possessing the characteristics associated with this disorder experiences a life-changing encounter with God:

The Story of Paul

"Saul, Saul, why do you persecute me?" With these words, Saul was introduced to the risen Christ, and his life forever changed.

Saul of Tarsus was trained under Gamaliel, the leading Pharisee of his day. Being an achiever, at the head of his class, Saul was likely being groomed to become the successor to Gamaliel. Saul's Jewish heritage and achievements brought him great recognition. He not only endeavored to obey the laws of the Old Testament (over 600), but he also endeavored to obey the Oral Law (over 6,000 in number)!

In Philippians 3 and Galatians 1, we get a glimpse of his accomplishments and passion for his beliefs. In Galatians 1, for example, he stated, "For you have heard of my previous way of life in Judaism, how intensely I persecuted the church of God and tried to destroy it. I was advancing in Judaism beyond many Jews of my own age and was extremely zealous for the traditions of my fathers" (Gal. 1:13–14). Certainly, in his day no one was more committed to his beliefs or tenacious in pursuing them than Saul.

Saul was "breathing out murderous threats" against the Christians, as stated in Acts 9:1. However, an amazing thing happened on the way to Damascus. When Christ addressed Saul, his beliefs changed in an instant. Saul's name was changed to Paul, and he became a staunch advocate of the grace of God extended to all through the death and resurrection of Jesus Christ. Once hating and destroying the Gentiles with a vengeance, Paul became a missionary to the Gentiles, willing to give his life for his faith.

In his life as a Pharisee, Saul could have been said to embody the characteristics of the achiever, with his conscientious dedication to his training and beliefs. It is also evident that his zeal reflects a compulsive, perfectionistic mentality in which anger and the need to control dominate. We have also seen these traits in obsessive-compulsive personality disorder, and while this is not the terminology used in the New Testament, Saul can be seen as manifesting the characteristics typical of obsessive-compulsive personality disorder.

What changed him? Nothing less than the unconditional love of God, and thus an experience with God's grace so profound that he was never the same. Paul spoke of this love in 1 Corinthians 13. How ironic that Saul, whose life was filled with hatred, was later to become known as Paul, author of this famous passage on love.

Spiritual Needs of the Individual
with Obsessive-Compulsive Personality Disorder:
Fruit of the Spirit—Patience

Experiencing God's unconditional love and acceptance can transform the life of an individual with obsessive-compulsive personality disorder. Which fruit of the Spirit can most minister to the hearts of these people? The fruit of patience. Paul wrote, "Love is patient" (1 Cor. 13:4). Paul probably demonstrated patience in his life most spectacularly in his behavior that is just the opposite of perfectionism—his tenacious dedication to grace, acceptance without works of any kind.

Those with this personality disorder desperately need patience with themselves and others. A prescription for developing patience is not meant to trivialize the ongoing struggles an individual with this personality disorder experiences on a daily basis. However, if those with obsessive-compulsive personality disorder can, over time, grasp the significance of God's unconditional love for them and learn to become more patient with their humanness (and the humanness of others), their lives can become meaningful and joyous.

The individual with obsessive-compulsive personality disorder, in order to become fully human, must experience the unconditional love and acceptance of God, for this is the basis for developing self-esteem. As power, almost certainly, was used inappropriately by their caretakers or other significant people in their lives in order to control them, they need to reclaim their own God-given power in an environment of unconditional love and acceptance in which there is safety and the consistent presence of trustworthy people. As the person with this disorder can be abrasive and critical, this is no easy task for those who are in contact with them. In fact, they may provoke others intentionally to test if a person will abandon them if they are found not to be "perfect."

Others will need to set carefully negotiated limits and boundaries with the person with obsessive-compulsive personality disorder. While individuals with this disorder tend to seek constant reassurances because of their insecurities, they need to learn to rely on their own perceptions and trust in their abilities to function competently.

Most obsessives will willingly admit to having difficulty expressing emotions, being perfectionistic and "hoarding" objects, although they may not understand their current interpersonal problems arising out of obsessive-compulsive personality disorder. The goal of therapy with these individuals is to help them change their assumptions so that their behaviors and emotions will change.[22]

This is not to say that questioning and even giving up the faulty assumptions that obsessive-compulsives have about themselves and others is a painless process. Rather, it is often excruciating, frequently causing more anxiety than they had experienced previously. Only with a great deal of patience and persistence on the part of the person with obsessive-compulsive personality disorder and those in contact with them, will emotions and behaviors yield to change.

Faulty advice was once given to pastors and counselors in working with obsessive-compulsives, taking control of the person's life and demanding their conformity, in order to "cure" them.[23] It is difficult to imagine worse advice, for individuals with this disorder have been previously abused by excessive control placed on them by others, rendering them powerless. Freedom is to be found in challenging conformity and questioning the faulty beliefs that have enslaved them.

How to Help

As a friend, coworker, or pastor, you can help the person with obsessive-compulsive personality disorder. Consider these suggestions.

1. Look past the "prickly," perfectionistic exterior. A vulnerable, terrified person is behind the facade.
2. Prove yourself to be trustworthy over time. Only after you have proven yourself as a person of integrity can you help them gradually challenge their false beliefs about themselves, others, and God.

3. Be honest in your communications. Never use manipulation by fear or guilt to motivate them, for this continues the pattern of emotional abuse used in the past by those who sought to control them.

4. When decisions are made that will affect them, include them (if at all possible) in the decision-making process, for they need to feel a sense of control in order to feel safe.

5. Acknowledge and show appreciation for their efforts and contributions, while also setting clear limits on their expectations of you.

6. Give them permission to be imperfect and yet accountable for the expectations they place on themselves and others.

7. Show yourself to be a safety net they can count on when they choose to take the risk to be emotionally vulnerable or to try something new.

8. Volunteer to be a reality check (at least initially) for them. They need others who can see life more in perspective and confirm that a task completed is "good enough" and does not have to be done perfectly. In time, you will want to back off, helping them to learn to make the decision of "good enough" for themselves, trusting their own perceptions.

9. Emphasize God's grace and help them see God as a partner in life. Avoid terms such as "surrendering your life to God" or "giving God control of your life." These emotionally abused individuals have a difficult time believing that God is trustworthy; try not to use a "power play" to control them.

10. If you feel an individual could have obsessive-compulsive personality disorder, recommend therapy. Cognitive-behavioral therapy is a good option.

♦ Two ♦

The Entertainer and Histrionic Personality Disorder

Personality Portrait of the Entertainer

*A*t any celebration, follow the sound of laughter and you will most likely find an entertainer at the center of the festivities surrounded by others. They are lots of fun to be around; an almost indispensable part of any gathering, they lift the spirits of those around them with their stories, jokes, and clever anecdotes.

The entertainer is blessed with a fun-loving spirit and a desire to give joy to others. Their sense of humor is healing. Life becomes "lighter" in their presence. They are demonstrative and affectionate people, with wonderful imaginations and an ability to view everyday occurrences in new ways. Entertainers express their emotions freely and make others feel at ease in openly expressing their emotions as well, whether joy or sorrow.[1] Being in the presence of the entertainer is fun and exciting as even the most mundane aspects of life become comical and "larger than life" when they are telling a story.

The Entertainer Versus Histrionic Personality Disorder

When personality traits are viewed as being on a continuum, on one end of the continuum is the healthy, positive expression of enjoyment of life, which the entertainer desires to experience and share with others. However, on the other end of the continuum, the fun-loving, desirable traits of the entertainer have been distorted and eclipsed by the presence of a pleasure-driven existence that is extreme and self-centered. When this occurs, the individual may be said to be suffering from histrionic personality disorder.

Persons with histrionic personality disorder crave fun. In fact, it becomes their sole pursuit, and they cannot tolerate any activity that does not place them at the center of a fun-filled existence. They are miserable when they are not being entertained or entertaining others. They believe they are entitled to live a privileged existence with others playing supporting roles. Individuals with histrionic personality disorder expect others to be amused and impressed by their antics, and they routinely manipulate others to do the work, while they play through life. Millon states, "The histrionic is a bottomless pit into which esteem and tribute may be poured."[2]

Histrionics are irresponsible and clever in getting others to believe they are privileged to be doing the histrionic's fair share of the work. The story of Tom Sawyer, in which others pay him to do his work, is a good illustration of the histrionic's approach to getting a job done. While entertainers certainly exaggerate their storytelling, the person with histrionic personality disorder regularly distorts the truth for the purpose of controlling others, commonly manipulating them with fear and guilt, yet smiling all the while. When a person with a histrionic personality disorder is smiling, it is often not a genuine expression of friendship or happiness. With their smile, they commonly mask a "hidden agenda" of control.

Betsy's Story

Betsy hugged Lucy and exclaimed, "I just love you! We have so many laughs together, don't we?"

Watching them together, it would be difficult to believe that Betsy and Lucy had met one week ago. Betsy and her husband had just begun attending the church in the community to which they had recently moved. It seemed as if Betsy had just descended on the church, taking it by storm with her vivacious personality. She was often surrounded by ripples of laughter as she related her hilarious antics of the past week. She flitted from group to group, young and old alike, dispensing hugs and laughs.

For the weary pastor and his wife, Betsy's presence at the church seemed like a minor miracle. She seemed to rejuvenate the members, entertaining them and lending a compassionate ear. However, the honeymoon did not last. Over time, while Betsy and her husband did not choose to join the church and become a part of any ministry within the church, Betsy demanded more and more time of the pastor, his wife, and other members. Betsy's need to discuss prayer requests, which she passed along from her many acquaintances, kept the whole congregation busy and kept her permanently at the center of everyone's attention. Minor occurrences became full-scale tragedies when Betsy related them. Members in the congregation began to complain to the pastor that he was neglecting other parishioners, for a great deal of his time was somehow spent "Betsy-related."

One evening she placed a frantic call to the head of the telephone prayer chain. "It's my son!" she cried. "Please pray for him. Since my grandson was born, we don't even see him or the baby each week. We stop at their house, and we just don't feel welcome. Now my daughter-in-law has decided to have them move two hours away! I can't stand it! It's all her fault! We do our best, and she just doesn't seem to want to be part of the family!"

Betsy frequently complained about her daughter-in-law's lack of spirituality and bemoaned her son's lack of spending extended periods of time visiting with her. In reality, in sheer frustration her son and daughter-in-law had chosen to move to another state to escape the constant calls, visits, and demands Betsy made on their time. While Betsy claimed to have a loving, close relationship with her son, it was superficial. Her son felt he always had to compete with Betsy's myriad of friends, whom Betsy treated with the same degree of affection as family members.

While they may appear to be gregarious and charming, individuals with a histrionic personality disorder are permanently "on," needing to be front and center stage at all times. They are playing a role rather than genuinely being themselves. Individuals with histrionic personality disorder play whichever role will get them what they desire, and they are capable of dramatically switching from a helpless, victim role with tears to a strong, in-charge person who possesses razor-sharp intellect, capable of defeating any opponent. The reason they are able to change demeanor so quickly is because they are indeed "acting the part" rather than genuinely experiencing the emotions they portray. While it would be easy to assume that they feel emotions deeply, persons with histrionic personality disorder simply are not able to do so. In fact, they experience little genuine emotion, perhaps due to repressed emotions of anger and fear locked inside their smiling exterior. Sadly, behind their smiles they are miserable.

Criteria for Histrionic Personality Disorder

The DSM-IV lists the criteria for the histrionic personality disorder as follows:

A pervasive pattern of excessive emotionality and attention seeking, beginning by early adulthood and present in a variety of contexts, as indicated by five (or more) of the following:

1. is uncomfortable in situations in which he or she is not the center of attention
2. interaction with others is often characterized by inappropriate sexually seductive or provocative behavior
3. displays rapidly shifting and shallow expression of emotions
4. consistently uses physical appearance to draw attention to self
5. has a style of speech that is excessively impressionistic and lacking in detail
6. shows self-dramatization, theatricality, and exaggerated expression of emotion
7. is suggestible, i.e., easily influenced by others or circumstances
8. considers relationships to be more intimate than they actually are[3]

The person with histrionic personality disorder believes he or she is not capable of coping with life's challenges. However, unlike the person with dependent personality disorder, who is openly self-doubting and passive, the histrionic deals with the situation in a more pragmatic fashion.[4] They actively seek others who will take care of them, commonly selecting more passive individuals whom they can control emotionally. Ironically, they manipulate other people into feeling dependent on them for the affirmation they are so good at providing. They are master manipulators, excellent at "honing in" on others' vulnerabilities and capitalizing on them. Their favorite target is an individual who is hurting, and thus emotionally needy. Millon states:

Histrionic personalities actively solicit the interest of others through a series of seductive ploys that are likely to assure receipt of the admiration and esteem they need. Toward these ends histrionics develop an exquisite sensitivity to the moods and thoughts of those they wish to please. This hyperalertness enables them to quickly assess what maneuvers will succeed in attaining the ends they desire.... Unlike dependent personalities, who anchor themselves usually to only one object of attachment, the histrionic tends to be lacking in fidelity and loyalty. The dissatisfaction with single attachments, combined with a need for constant stimulation and attention, results in a seductive, dramatic, and capricious pattern of personal relationships.[5]

Another difference between dependent and histrionic personality disorders is that while the dependent experiences difficulty *saying* no to others' inappropriate expectations and demands, the histrionic, in contrast, has difficulty *hearing* no, thus violating the emotional boundaries of others through their manipulative persuasion.[6]

These intelligent and capable individuals feel the need to resort to such tactics in order to feel a sense of safety and control in life. They were trained to believe that they are incapable and must depend on others to meet their needs.

How are individuals with histrionic personality disorder able to accomplish their deception? They are often people with above-average intelligence who can masterfully make another individual feel important, special, and affirmed. Unfortunately, the church is often one of the best hiding places for individuals with histrionic personality disorder. They use "God talk" and feigned interest in others to get what they want. They are usually the center of attention in a church with their charismatic personality and initially, at least, are highly regarded by others for their "spirituality," as they appear to be genuinely caring and compassionate. They often change churches when their audience begins to catch on that their charming, often melodramatic style is not accompanied by a consistent desire to serve others, for example, by committing to teach Sunday school or serve on a committee. Their circle of friends changes frequently as well, as people discover that they are being used. However, only the most discerning individuals can see through their smiling masks to the hurting individual inside. Although deeply wounded at the core of their lives, those with histrionic personality disorder do not usually endeavor to change their behavior. They simply find another audience who can meet their needs. Only when they feel that their options have run out do they often choose to get help, confronting their pain and endeavoring to live an authentic life of faithfulness to God and others.

Belief System of Individuals with Histrionic Personality Disorder

The belief system of the individual with histrionic personality disorder is aptly summarized as follows:

1. I am an interesting, exciting person.
2. In order to be happy, I need other people to pay attention to me.
3. Unless I entertain or impress people, I am nothing.
4. If I don't keep others engaged with me, they won't like me.
5. The way to get what I want is to dazzle or amuse people.
6. If people don't respond very positively to me, they are rotten.
7. It is awful if people ignore me.
8. I should be the center of attention.
9. I don't have to bother to think things through—I can go by my "gut" feeling.
10. If I entertain people, they will not notice my weaknesses.
11. I cannot tolerate boredom.
12. If I feel like doing something, I should go ahead and do it.
13. People will pay attention only if I act in extreme ways.
14. Feelings and intuition are much more important than rational thinking and planning.[7]

Feelings Experienced by Others

What emotions do others experience when in the presence of a person with histrionic personality disorder? When meeting a person with histrionic personality disorder, typically one feels flattered by the attention of the individual and may be easily impressed by the person's warmth, vivacious nature, and attractiveness. These individuals are entertaining and seductive, and one is drawn to them.[8] In their presence, at least initially, typically one feels very good.

Over time, however, "the charm seems to wear thin, and they gradually are seen as overly demanding and in need of constant reassurance."[9] The "mixed messages" they use to control and manipulate others create feelings of confusion and anger at being used and betrayed. Histrionics typically demand trust yet do not try to earn it. Because they are so good at manipulating others' emotions, those in a relationship with them commonly feel at fault for questioning the histrionic's motives and blame themselves for the histrionic's lack of faithfulness by feeling unworthy of true devotion. One often feels inferior in the presence of the histrionic and dependent on the individual for emotional support.

Histrionics intentionally attempt to keep others confused and off balance emotionally in order to control them, and they avoid allowing others to set healthy emotional boundaries with them, thus encouraging unhealthy relationships. Frequently, those in a long-term relationship feel as if they may be crazy, for the histrionic denies the dramatic shift in emotions and the subtle mixed messages they use to control others. The histrionic's true intentions are often hidden behind a facade of kindness and supposed geniuneness. When assertively confronted, histrionics often respond with fury.

Individuals in long-term relationships with histrionics may feel trapped. Since healthy emotional boundaries have not been respected, they frequently feel exploited and violated. When a histrionic replaces them with a new fan, as is commonly the case, an individual commonly experiences great rage at the histrionic's unfaithfulness.

Those with histrionic personality disorder place great emphasis on appearances. They frequently engage in superficial relationships, and thus their acquaintances may only see them in a positive, caring light, feeling great admiration for them. This is intensely frustrating to the individual in a long-term relationship with them, because they are so adored by others who do not know them for who they truly are.

Cloud and Townsend state in *Safe People*, "An unsafe person may make you feel good—yet wound you emotionally."[10] Ironically, those with histrionic personality disorder, while making people in superficial relationships with them feel special, nevertheless deal in deception and therefore are not able to maintain truly healthy relationships. Cloud and Townsend remark in referring to unsafe people, "In a relationship, honesty is the bedrock foundation of a safe relationship. To the degree that there is deception, there is danger."[11]

Factors in the Development of Histrionic Personality Disorder: Nature Versus Nurture

While histrionic personality disorder has typically been associated more with women than men (sex role stereotypes being a factor), both women and men can have histrionic personality disorder. Is histrionic personality disorder created by a genetic predisposition, family background, or cultural expectations? While biological components in the development of the histrionic personality disorder continue to be explored,[12] one must consider environmental factors as well. "Female histrionics (as well as some of the males) seem to have been rewarded from an early age for cuteness, physical attractiveness, and charm rather than for competence or for any endeavor requiring systematic thought and planning. The more 'macho' male histrionics have learned to play an extreme masculine role, being rewarded for virility, toughness, and power rather than actual competence or problem-solving ability. Understandably, then, both male and female histrionics learn to focus attention on the playing of roles and 'performing' for others."[13]

Millon states:

> The parents of the future histrionic rarely punish their children, they distribute rewards only for what they approve and admire, but they often fail to bestow these rewards even when the child behaves acceptably. . . . If a child such as this learns that the achievement of rewards is dependent on fulfilling the expectations and desires of others, he or she will develop a set of instrumental behaviors designed to please others and thereby elicit these rewards. However, if these behaviors succeed sometimes but not always, the child will persist in using them well beyond all reason—until they do succeed, which they eventually will.... Future histrionics learn to look to others for the judgment of whether their efforts justify approval.[14]

Millon offers two additional features of family life which can contribute to an individual's developing histrionic personality disorder: first, parents who are histrionic themselves (likely having had their own emotional boundaries violated) and thus the children mimic the parents' behavior; and second, sibling rivalry in which the child believes that the only way to earn the attention of the parents is through "cuteness, charm, attractiveness, and seductiveness."[15]

Societal Expectations

Our society tends to reinforce the personality traits associated with histrionic personality disorder for females, and thus cultural expectations communicated through the family and others are a factor in the development of histrionic personality disorder. Sex role expectations were subtly (and sometimes not so subtly) taught to members of the baby boomer generation. For example, the *Lucy Show* and Fred and Wilma Flintstone versions of male/female roles and relationships communicated societal expectations. Women were expected to get their needs met not through honest communication, but through manipulative, overly emotional behavior. They were not to "worry their pretty little heads" about anything but rather to expect a male to rescue them. Typically, women were expected to be taken care of financially by their husbands but not understood by them. Real friendship was not seen to be commonly experienced between husband and wife, but they were to experience a mutually accommodating relationship. And above all, feigned helplessness on the part of the woman was the number one rule of the game. Does this sound like the characteristics associated with histrionic personality disorder? Absolutely! Cultural expectations of female personality traits and behaviors can be a significant factor in the development of not only histrionic personality disorder but also dependent personality disorder, which we will discuss in the next chapter.

While society has tended to reinforce the image of attention-seeking, histrionic-type behavior as acceptable and even desirable for females, what accounts for the fact that only some women develop this disorder? A primary consideration is that of family background, for dysfunctional family rules can prevent individuals from becoming fully functioning adults. As we have discussed, histrionics can emerge from families in which they have been encouraged to remain childish in their perspective because it was in the best interests of the family for them to remain in that state. Also, as those with histrionic personality disorder do not respect others' boundaries, likely their own boundaries as children were not respected, which is indicative of abuse.

Role of the Church

The church can also unwittingly encourage and reinforce the characteristics associated with histrionic personality disorder. The histrionics' overly emotional appeal can be seen as a desired trait for bringing new people into the church and for evangelization. The way they immediately bond with strangers, treating them with the same affection as family members, can be viewed by some as superspiritual. In fact, histrionics tend to dazzle others with their personality and may indeed bring a number of individuals into the church and keep them there by entertaining them and taking an intense interest in their needs. However, discerning individuals begin to realize that the "God talk" does not match their actions over time, and that their interest in others is calculated to carry out their own agenda.

While individuals experiencing personality disorders such as obsessive-compulsive personality disorder or dependent personality disorder may seek professional help because of the distress they feel, this is not typically the case for individuals with histrionic personality disorder. They seek help usually only when they have experienced "a period of social disapproval or deprivation," and anxiety or depression may be evident. However, histrionics tend to become bored easily and therefore rarely follow through with long-term therapy.[16]

Also, as they consistently look to others to fulfill their needs, as soon as another substitute enters their life who promises to give them the attention and approval they seek, they typically feel little need to do any work to change the behaviors associated with histrionic personality disorder, rather resorting to old, familiar patterns of behavior which have previously been rewarded by others.

Hope and Help: The Story of Mark

Is there hope for the individual suffering from histrionic personality disorder? Yes! Let's look at the life of Mark, a biblical character whose life was transformed by a relationship with God.

Tradition has it that the mother of Mark owned the upper room in which Jesus celebrated the last supper (cf. Acts 12:12 with Mark 14:13–15; Acts 1:13; 4:1). Mark, born into a wealthy family, enjoyed feasts and entertainment. He may have initially followed Jesus for the fun and excitement that Jesus' miracles brought. However, he also seems to be the young man who fled from the garden of Gethsemene, avoiding associating with Jesus in his time of suffering.

He repeated his pattern when he abandoned Paul on their first missionary journey (Acts 13). Consequently, Paul refused to take him on his second missionary journey, taking Silas instead. Years later, at the end of his life, Paul asked for Mark to join him because Mark had now become profitable (faithful) to the ministry. Mark responded to Paul's request and remained faithful to God. Ultimately, Mark wrote the second Gospel, showing he had persevered in his faithfulness.

Thus, the profile that emerges of Mark is that of a young man who was initially enamored with Christ's miracles and the crowds and attention it brought but was not faithful. Through the power of the Holy Spirit, that faithlessness was replaced with fidelity.

Spiritual Needs of the Individual with Histrionic Personality Disorder: Fruit of the Spirit—Faithfulness

Those with histrionic personality disorder desperately need to experience the unconditional love of God. They need to come to grips with the fact that one does not have to perform, to be charming or entertaining to merit God's love. The particular fruit of the spirit that can transform them into honest, authentic human beings, is faithfulness. They must experience the faithfulness of God and learn to become faithful to others. These people possess great gifts of creativity through which they can deeply touch their world. However, their pleasure-driven, self-centered existence has eclipsed their strength, that of being fun-loving people who deeply enjoy life and who wish to share this joy with others.

Committing to the hard work of learning to be faithful is difficult for them, for they often are able simply to find a new audience, which temporarily eases the pain they feel. However, God is faithful and often places people in their lives to confront them with the truth and allow them to experience the consequences of their behavior. When they are willing to face the truth and become faithful, self-reliant individuals, they often have great impact, leaving a legacy of joy.

How to Help

If you are in a relationship with a person with histrionic personality disorder as a pastor, coworker, or friend, here are some suggestions:

1. Look behind the facade to the wounded souls. Help them to become authentic human beings by not rescuing them from the consequences of their actions.
2. Set clear boundaries with the person with histrionic personality disorder and stick with those boundaries.
3. Be mindful of the individual's pattern of interpersonal relationships. While he or she may make you feel loved and affirmed, be aware that the histrionic does not sustain relationships. If you expect faithfulness, you will most likely be disappointed.

4. Remember that the histrionic typically has a hidden agenda. Confront them when they are manipulative. Bring them out in the open by asking questions rather than providing answers.

5. Depend on others for emotional support rather than on a histrionic. If he or she cannot hook you through being vulnerable to feelings of guilt, for example, it is more difficult for the histrionic to manipulate you.

6. Do not equate "God talk" and feigned interest in others with spirituality. Look to see if the individual has, over time, walked the walk, instead of just talking the talk.

7. Be wary when an individual has "church hopped" frequently or often has a new circle of friends.

8. For pastors, kindly, but firmly, refuse to give the histrionic any more of your time than you give other members.

9. Acknowledge their need for attention and approval by genuinely caring for them.

10. Help them develop the habits of honesty, self-reliance, and faithfulness by modeling, encouraging, and expecting these behaviors from them as well.

◆ Three ◆

The Follower and
Dependent Personality Disorder

"*F*riends forever" is the theme of the faithful follower. These devoted folks are loving, loyal friends through good and bad times. We can count on them to listen sympathetically to our problems and also share in our joys. Oldham and Morris are referring to these people when they say, "Devoted people are the ones who tell you, 'I'm happy if you're happy'—and mean it." They go on to say that these people are committed to their friends, considerate of others, and cooperative and respectful of authority.[1] These are easy people to be around. They do not really make demands and are just happy to be with you.

In churches, these individuals are good team players and hard workers. Serving faithfully on committees, they would rather follow than lead, and they are good at following through on directions given to them and persevering until a task is completed. The follower prefers to be behind the scenes rather than in the limelight and is not preoccupied with getting the accolades for what he or she does. They want everyone to be happy and work to be peacemakers.

We count ourselves fortunate indeed if we have one such friend on whom we can depend. They make us feel cared for and loved. They are sacrificial in giving their time, and we know we can count on them. What could be better?

The Faithful Follower Versus Dependent Personality Disorder

There is a point, however, along the continuum of personality traits, where rather than being a faithful follower, a healthy way to relate to others, one experiences an extreme, destructive form of fidelity to others which is healthy for neither the giver nor the receiver. In these cases, a frantic, clinging dependency on others reflects a sense of fear and helplessness. Dependent individuals view themselves as: "(1) controlled by people and external events, (2) powerless to influence the outcome of events, and therefore (3) not responsible for the consequences of their behavior."[2] Bornstein speaks of four components of dependence: (1) feeling the need of support and guidance from others; (2) believing themselves to be powerless and seeing others as powerful; (3) becoming anxious when they need to function independently; and (4) seeking help, guidance, and approval from others, yielding to others.[3] A dependent personality disorder involves an extreme, unhealthy, passive way of relating to others that emerges out of a faulty belief system.

Human beings share the common struggle of moving from a state of total dependence on others during infancy to a position of greater autonomy over the years, eventually (and ideally) becoming self-reliant, fully functioning adults. Healthy functioning also involves recognizing the interdependency which we all have on one another in the human family and being flexible in our behavior, depending on the situation involved. For example, as adults, when in the presence of a person viewed as an authority figure, such as a doctor or boss, we may defer to their knowledge, playing a more dependent role; while with our friends, we may debate views on a subject, showing independent ways of thinking and relating to one another. In times of stress, it is typical to play a more dependent role, as we may feel overwhelmed by life's demands or the circumstances in which we find ourselves. We are particularly vulnerable at these times and seek to have others take care of, or to nurture, us.

That is different from individuals with dependent personality disorder. Their behavior is consistently extreme in its dependency. Those with a dependent personality disorder do not possess flexibility in their relationships with others. They are stuck in a passive mode, allowing and expecting life to act on them. These people believe they are helpless and constantly feel the need to have a rescuer who will meet their needs, and without whom they feel they cannot survive emotionally and/or physically. They are prone to depression and anxiety due to their great feelings of being threatened and vulnerable in the world. They believe they must "bind themselves" to a strong person subordinating themselves to this person, and constantly trying to please and placate the "rescuer."[4] Oldham and Morris, in their book *The New Personality Self-Portrait*, equate the terms "dependent people" and "codependent."[5]

Dependent Personality Disorder and Histrionic Personality Disorder: Similarities and Differences

The dependent personality disorder and the histrionic personality disorder are seen as sharing the following characteristics: (1) these disorders are more stereotypically associated with females, although the conditions are not limited to females (cultural sex role expectations certainly play a major role in this occurrence); and (2) individuals with either of these disorders believe they cannot handle life on their own and look to others to meet their needs.

However, the way the individuals go about meeting these needs is different, depending on which personality disorder the person possesses. Individuals with dependent personality disorder passively look to others, hoping they will rescue them from disaster over which they believe they have no control. In contrast, those with histrionic personality disorder are active in pursuing rescuers. They do not leave anything to chance. While they believe they cannot handle life on their own, they also possess confidence that through their charm they can attract a rescuer through which their needs can be meet. Therefore, they do not commonly experience the depth of hopelessness, lack of control over life, and helplessness which characterize dependent personality disorder, unless they find they are unable to attract a rescuer to meet their needs.

Although individuals "with either histrionic personality disorder or dependent personality disorder may appear childlike and clinging," the person with dependent personality disorder is "less flamboyant, egocentric, and shallow" than the histrionic. "The individual with DPD (dependent personality disorder) tends to be passive, submissive, self-effacing, and docile; this contrasts with the actively manipulative, gregarious, charming, and seductive behaviors of the individual with histrionic personality disorder."[6]

There is one more significant difference between histrionic and dependent personality disorders. The individual with dependent personality disorder is faithful to a fault; that is, the individual remains faithful to the person perceived as a rescuer even when mistreated and abused by the individual. The histrionic has the opposite problem. The histrionic is not capable of being faithful to anyone and thus leaves a trail of casualties behind.

Kelly's Story

Kelly is a person with dependent personality disorder. The following letter to her husband summarizes her life:

> Dear Gary,
> Please come home! I'm sorry for making you angry. I know I make you drink because I haven't really been a good enough wife. I will try a lot harder. I can keep the house cleaner, and I'll do better keeping the kids quiet so you can sleep.
> I know it's my fault you are living with that woman from work. I'm sorry that I complained a lot about how many hours you work and the nights you go out. I'll try harder to be a better wife. I miss you so much!
> If you come home, everything will be OK. Please give me another chance. You know how much I need you.
> Love, Kelly

This person is obviously in pain. She gets involved in unhealthy relationships and feels powerless to improve her life. Kelly is afraid and depressed, feeling she can't function on her own. She is terrified of being alone and has tolerated inappropriate, and even abusive, behavior in order to have someone who is "strong" in her life, a person she believes will take care of her.

It is not difficult to identify a person with dependent personality disorder. The way a person carries himself/herself, as well as the voice, words, and mannerisms of the person, are all clues as to the presence of this disorder. Characteristically, these individuals lack self-confidence and tend to speak and move tentatively.[7] They are self-effacing and self-depreciating. As Millon states, "A clinging helplessness and a search for support and reassurance characterize them."[8] They endeavor neither to disturb nor to offend others to whom they have attached themselves. Oldham and Morris remark, "Despite all apparent evidence to the contrary, they honestly believe that they are inadequate in everything from looks to abilities to mental capacity. Underneath the smiling face of a dependent person lurks someone who has little or no confidence, coupled with a huge need for reassurance. This man or woman reaches out to gain self-esteem from other people."[9]

In order to please others, the person with dependent personality disorder may appear always to be cheerful. Therefore, others may not realize the internal suffering taking place behind the smile.[10] Those with dependent personality disorder are always afraid of losing their rescuer, whom they view as competent and strong.[11] If they lose their "life-support" person, they may well appear to be anxious, depressed, and overwhelmed.

Criteria for Dependent Personality Disorder

The DSM-IV lists the criteria for dependent personality disorder as follows:

A pervasive and excessive need to be taken care of that leads to submissive and clinging behavior and fears of separation, beginning by early adulthood and present in a variety of contexts, as indicated by five (or more) of the following:

1. has difficulty making everyday decisions without an excessive amount of advice and reassurance from others
2. needs others to assume responsibility for most major areas of his or her life
3. has difficulty expressing disagreement with others because of fear of loss of support or approval (Note: Does not include realistic fears of retribution)
4. has difficulty initiating projects or doing things on his or her own (because of a lack of self-confidence in judgment or abilities rather than a lack of motivation or energy)
5. goes to excessive lengths to obtain nurturance and support from others, to the point of volunteering to do things that are unpleasant
6. feels uncomfortable or helpless when alone because of exaggerated fears of being unable to care for himself or herself
7. urgently seeks another relationship as a source of care and support when a close relationship ends
8. is unrealistically preoccupied with fears of being left to take care of himself or herself [12]

Belief System of Individuals with Dependent Personality Disorder

Every person possesses a core set of beliefs about himself/herself and others which, in turn, determine his/her actions. The belief system of the individual with dependent personality disorder is summarized as follows:

1. I am needy and weak.
2. I need somebody around, available at all times to help me to carry out what I need to do or in case something bad happens.
3. My helper can be nurturant, supportive, and confident—if he or she wants to be.
4. I am helpless when I'm left on my own.
5. I am basically alone—unless I can attach myself to a stronger person.
6. The worst possible thing would be to be abandoned.
7. If I am not loved, I will always be unhappy.
8. I must do nothing to offend my supporter or helper.
9. I must be subservient in order to maintain his or her good will.
10. I must maintain access to him or her at all times.
11. I should cultivate as intimate a relationship as possible.
12. I can't make decisions on my own.
13. I can't cope as other people can.
14. I need others to help me make decisions or tell me what to do.[13]

Individuals with dependent personality disorder are easy targets for abusive behavior because they believe they are at the mercy of life and do not have the resources to take control of their life, just as certain groups of people experience a higher risk of abuse due to age, situation in life, or physical difficulties. Bornstein states, "The dependency of a child, a nonworking spouse, or an elderly parent on a family member increases the likelihood that the dependent person will become a victim of physical or psychological abuse."[14]

Unfortunately, the person with dependent personality disorder is also at risk of abusing others when placed in a caretaking situation. They do not believe they are capable of taking care of themselves, let alone anyone else. Feeling overwhelmed, they may submit others to physical or psychological abuse. Bornstein states, "Clearly, assuming the caretaker role requires that one allow one's own dependency needs to go unmet. While this may be possible for the individual who does not have a dependent personality orientation, it will be extremely difficult (and frustrating) for the dependent person to relinquish the passive, dependent role in favor of an active, caretaking stance in familial relationships."[15]

Feelings Experienced by Others

The feelings experienced by others when in the presence of an individual with a personality disorder can be an excellent alarm system for detecting its presence. How does one feel when in the presence of an individual with dependent personality disorder? Just like other personality disorders such as histrionic or obsessive-compulsive, first impressions and casual acquaintances may experience different feelings than those in a long-term relationship with a person who has a personality disorder.

Initially, because persons with dependent personality disorder appear so needy and docile, they elicit feelings of sympathy. One wants to help these people, and some fall easily into a rescuer role. They are so appreciative of attention and help that one feels important and special because of the impression of being so needed. However, over time, others commonly experience great feelings of frustration. While listening attentively to others' suggestions as to how they could take control of their lives, individuals with dependent personality disorder do not typically follow through by taking action which would help them actually improve their lives. They rather choose to stay in a dependent state (out of fear), and others weary of this. People become exasperated with the individual's passive way of dealing with life and are tempted to say, "Just do something!"

A resulting feeling of helplessness is thus commonly experienced by others in a relationship with a person with dependent personality disorder. The dependent clings desperately to a rescuer, and when it is evident that the person is not working toward becoming a self-reliant, fully functioning individual, the rescuer often feels trapped. Feeling controlled by the individual with dependent personality disorder, rescuers are often faced with the option of ending the relationship and thus suffering the guilt heaped on them by the dependent or remaining in a permanent "parent-child" role with the individual.

Factors in the Development of Dependent Personality Disorder: Nature Versus Nurture

Exploring the causes of this disorder will help us understand people with dependent personality disorder. Genetic predisposition, the experience of chronic illness, sex role stereotypes and parenting styles are all possible factors in the development of dependent personality disorder.[16] Some believe that an individual may possess a genetic predisposition to develop dependent personality disorder. Oldham and Morris state, "Submissive behavior may be a genetically determined trait, predisposing some children to develop this personality disorder if they encounter certain kinds of stresses."[17]

Home Environment

Environment plays a great role in determining how people view themselves and others, and family background is commonly seen as a factor in the development of dependent personality disorder. What is this environment like? Two types of parenting styles can result in a child's developing dependent personality disorder. The first style involves overprotective parents. Due to the words and actions of such parents, these children come to view the world as a hostile place from which only the parent (or another strong authority figure) can protect them. These children believe they do not have sufficient resources to protect or take care of themselves and, therefore, must be in the presence of a strong person on whom they can rely at all times. Life is experienced as threatening, and they believe they have little control over what happens to them.

The second parenting style which can result in a child's developing dependent personality disorder is authoritarianism. Here the parents are intrusive and discourage independent thought or actions. The child is blocked from developing a sense of autonomy needed for becoming an independent, full-functioning adult in the future.[18] The child learns that the parent's words and actions are not to be questioned and the consequences of independent thinking or actions involve significant pain physically or emotionally. The child is placed in a powerless situation. These children do not develop the skills needed to become self-reliant and view themselves as weak and incapable, looking to others to make decisions for them.

Parental overprotectiveness and/or authoritarianism may thus result in a child's developing dependent personality disorder; when occurring simultaneously this further predisposes a child to develop this personality disorder. Bornstein states, "Parental overprotectiveness and authoritarianism serve simultaneously to: (1) reinforce dependent behaviors in children of both sexes and (2) prevent the child from developing independent, autonomous behaviors (since the parents do not permit the child to engage in the kinds of trial-and-error learning that are involved in developing a sense of independence and mastery during childhood)."[19]

In order to be healthy psychologically, children must feel safe in their environment and believe that those around them are trustworthy. While the goal of effective parenting is to watch a child grow into an independent, confident adult through a nurturing environment, overprotective and/or authoritarian parents (who may have been abused emotionally themselves) are unable to foster independence and confidence in their children. Dependents come to believe that others hold the key to their survival. Because they have not been allowed or encouraged to set healthy emotional and physical boundaries, their spirit is crushed. They feel they have no control over their lives and frequently experience despair. This has enormous consequences for interpersonal relationships as well as developing a spiritual relationship with God, for their interpretation of the words "surrendering to God," or "doing the will of God," or "being submissive to God's will" involves what they perceive as an extension of what they have experienced in the past—relinquishing all power to others—rather than viewing a relationship with God as the partnership between a loving God and themselves. God is seen as "one more" in a succession of controllers, a "divine puppeteer."

Societal Expectations

The family unit reflects societal expectations as well. What part do societal expectations play in the development of dependent personality disorder? Much has been written about the stereotypic personality traits associated with sex role expectations. The traits involving both dependent personality disorder and histrionic personality disorder are those associated with sex-role stereotypic behavior for females in our society. While only a limited number of individuals meet the criteria for dependent personality disorder (female and male), societal expectations concerning dependency can be a factor in developing dependent personality disorder for those who are already predisposed to this condition through possible genetic predisposition and/or family background.

From the moment we are born, our lives are shaped by others' expectations. As we grow, we attempt to sort through these expectations to form our own beliefs about how the ideal woman or man is supposed to act, look, and behave in our society. Departing from our society's commonly held expectations of male and female roles is painful. What feminine characteristics have been traditionally valued in our society? Generally, it is a picture of a gentle, loving, kind, self-sacrificing individual. Not surprisingly, when carried to an extreme, these are also the traits of dependent personality disorder. Women have also traditionally been expected to exhibit the characteristics associated with histrionic personality disorder: manipulative, self-centered, appearance-oriented and overly emotional.

Society has taught women who they must be to survive in the culture and then labeled them as inferior and berated them for learning their lessons well. Schaef discusses this phenomenon regarding the training which culture provides for females in the development of certain personality traits and expected behaviors. She remarks that "family, school and church teach us not to form boundaries. Their message is: Think what you are told to think. Feel what you are told to feel. See what you are told to see."[20]

Expectations of male and female behavior and roles were communicated to members of the baby boomer generation not only by families, churches, and schools but also by exposure to the media. Those were the days of *Father Knows Best* and *Leave It to Beaver*. Of course, this is a factor in shaping our image of the ideal man and woman and expectations regarding relationships.

These television programs basically involved caucasian, middle-class families. Could it be that the "learned helplessness" characteristic of dependency may be a primarily caucasian, middle- to upper-class phenomenon involving women? One African-American woman stated, "African-American women have always been raised to believe they are capable of taking care of themselves." Socioeconomically, mainly middle- and upper-class women were given the option of not working outside the home after World War II. Women were such a vital workforce during the war, but the return of the men after the war displaced them. Certainly these displaced workers were different in many ways from the women these men left during the war. The impact of World War II as it relates to dependency issues would make an interesting study.

Is dependency still romanticized and idealized in our society today, particularly in regard to male-female relationships? Schaef remarks that the "suffering, clinging love"—perhaps a romantic novel version—has the "same elements as an addictive relationship."[21] These individuals must cling to one another out of desperate need. Also, in examining the influence of society on one's perception of ideal womanhood and manhood, Kasl has stated that a power imbalance in families can lead to dependency.[22] When marriage is not seen as an equal partnership between two individuals who each bring both strengths and weaknesses, talents and capabilities for taking care of and nurturing themselves and others, they are at risk of developing a dependent, unhealthy relationship.

Role of the Church

The church itself can unknowingly reinforce beliefs toward oneself and others which are unspiritual and unhealthy by creating and perpetuating a dependency mentality in its members, thus becoming a factor in the development of dependent personality disorder. This unhealthy form of dependency may involve either those in authority in the church (deacons, elders, pastors, or other respected spiritual leaders) or a faulty view of God.

One aspect of spirituality is showing humility involving an openness to learn from others. In showing deference to the knowledge of those in authority in the church, individuals may develop an unhealthy dependence when church leaders expect others to play a subservient role in knowledge about spiritual matters, which is actually based on power rather than on love. These individuals, while appearing to be spiritual, are actually power hungry and demand obedience to their version of truth. Many people are easily exploited by spiritually arrogant individuals who claim to have a corner on the truth through a perceived superior relationship with God. Children are especially vulnerable in this regard. They may be taught that their church's beliefs are the only correct ones, and they must believe and behave as those in authority in the church. Thus, children are not encouraged to ask questions or to disagree. Harsh, dogmatic, legalistic church settings create dependency problems as people become passive recipients of the church's teachings, with the authority figures in the church regulating the beliefs and behaviors of its members.

Commonly, a view of God as supreme Judge is consistent with the teaching in these churches. Thus, members may not only form an unhealthy, dependent relationship on church leaders, but they may also form a clinging dependency on a "powerful, vengeful God," whom they are terrified of offending. A loving, trusting relationship with a God who loves and accepts them unconditionally is not part of their experience. These individuals believe they must rely totally on a God who cannot be satisfied, and they see their powerlessness as a sign of spirituality.

Hope and Help: The Story of Mary Magdalene

In contrast, let's look at the life of Mary Magdalene, who experienced liberation from a life of dependency due to the power of Jesus Christ.

The healing of Mary Magdalene, who was oppressed by evil spirits, was a magnificent expression of God's love and power. Delivered from these demons by Jesus, her healing seems to have involved many different aspects: physical, emotional, mental, and spiritual (Luke 8:2). Consequently, out of gratitude and love, she chose to travel with Jesus and his disciples during their evangelistic ministry. Clearly, she was close to Jesus and was one of the women present at his crucifixion (Mark 15:40; Matt. 27:56; John 19:25).

Mary Magdalene must have experienced great grief at Jesus' death. Visiting his tomb several days later, she found it to be empty. Jesus showed his great love by appearing first to her after his resurrection from the dead. Mary Magdalene must have relied heavily on Jesus, as she is portrayed as "clinging to him." Jesus not only freed her from demon possession and all that involved but in a great act of love and compassion freed her from a clinging dependence on him as well. Either way, clinging to demons or clinging excessively to Jesus is a manifestation of Mary's dependent personality. Jesus told her to cease clinging to him, releasing her from the dependency of low self-esteem and feelings of inadequacy, and encouraging her to take charge of her own life, claiming the power which his love affords (John 20:1–18).

Spiritual Needs of the Individual with Dependent Personality Disorder: Fruit of the Spirit—Meekness

Mary Magdalene certainly must have seen firsthand the meekness Jesus demonstrated in his life. He used wisdom and demonstrated power under control (the expression of meekness). Jesus was Mary Magdalene's role model in claiming one's power and using it to help others.

The word *meekness* is easily misunderstood to be synonymous with *weakness*. This is not the case. Meekness is more accurately an attitude of power under control, taught and demonstrated by Jesus. Jesus was not a wimp. His cleansing of the temple clearly showed strong, decisive action. What is meekness then? The instance in which Jesus did not answer his accusers is thought to be the greatest example of Jesus' meekness. Was he afraid, intimidated, or unable to answer his accusers? No. Rather, Jesus showed his wisdom, love, and power by not being baited by these individuals. This is an ultimate demonstration of Jesus' power under control, a true expression of meekness.

Individuals with dependent personality disorder need to discover the liberating, unconditional love of God and reclaim their God-given power to take charge of their lives. While they have perceived themselves as helpless and have demonstrated weakness, they need the fruit of the Spirit—meekness—in order to claim their birthright of power as God's children. Through meekness, respect of oneself and others is evident, and humility of spirit is best seen in a heart filled with gratitude for the many talents and capabilities God has placed in each soul. These gifts are to be used to impact the world with the love of Christ.

How to Help

If you are a friend, pastor, relative, or coworker of a person with dependent personality disorder, how can you help this individual? Here are some suggestions:

1. While we can all feel a great deal of sympathy for these wounded souls, we should resist the temptation to rescue them. They are capable, even though they don't feel they are. While rescuing may seem to be the obvious solution when they are in a situation they believe they cannot handle, it is not in their best interest to do so. In the long run, rescuing is detrimental to their becoming fully functioning adults.[23]

2. Lovingly, but firmly, help them evaluate their options and hold them accountable for following through.[24] Initially, begin encouraging them to make smaller, less significant decisions and thereby gain self-confidence. Even the decision of what to eat or wear may be troublesome for these individuals.

3. Expect them to try to pull you back into a rescuing role a number of times. Do not allow your emotions to overrule your better judgment. Try to detach yourself emotionally enough to see the bigger picture.

4. Set clear boundaries, and stick with them. The goal is to help the individual become a self-reliant, fully functioning person.

5. Endeavor to be a role model for the appropriate expression of emotions: joy, anger, fear, and sorrow.

6. Let them know you are a safe person with whom they can vent their emotions. Individuals with dependent personality disorder are terrified that others will abandon them if they offend them or let them know who they truly are.

7. People love to have someone go out of their way to please them. However, as Oldham and Morris state, "lovingly discourage their attempts to go too far out of their way to please you. Keep in mind that it's difficult not to take advantage of people who are very passive."[25] While certainly not done intentionally, examine whether you might

be participating unknowingly in behaviors which encourage or foster unhealthy dependency in these people.

8. Don't hesitate to recommend counseling for those you believe may have dependent personality disorder. It is not your responsibility, nor should you as a layperson try, to provide the therapy these individuals often need. If you are in a relationship with an individual with dependent personality disorder, participate in therapy with them if you are experiencing difficulties in your relationship.[26]

◆ Four ◆

The Star and Narcissistic Personality Disorder

*T*he roar of the crowd and applause are sweet music to the ears of the star. Vivacious and articulate, the star loves being the center of attention and readily admits to it! These people have charismatic personalities. Everyone wants to be a part of their world. They have marvelous self-esteem, believing in themselves and their abilities and assertively pursuing their dreams, while also respecting and valuing others.

The star has a magnetic quality that draws people to himself or herself. At ease when cast in a prominent role in life (and at their best in the limelight), these front-and-center-stage people are exciting to be with, viewing life fearlessly and welcoming spontaneity. They are free spirits and resist conformity; they radiate energetic creativity. Like the character Auntie Mame, the star views life as a sumptuous banquet and pities those who do not partake of the excitement and joy of life.

The Star Versus the Entertainer

The difference in attitudes or actions between the star and the entertainer is only a subtle difference in personality. Both like the limelight and enjoy an audience. However, the star exudes confidence and, with a "larger than life" persona, expects to attract others. These individuals do not always feel the need to entertain in order to draw others to themselves; they know their presence is enough. Entertainers, in contrast, do not display such confidence; in fact, their appeal may be in drawing others to themselves through humorous antics and stories that often play off their own weaknesses, rather than strengths; therefore, they often play a bungling, but loveable role. Both the star and the entertainer like people and thrive when they are at the center of attention.

The star has a great deal to give. Talented, ambitious, and possessing a great deal of influence, these people can inspire others to become involved in great causes to which they lend credence. Their confidence and way with words can profoundly motivate people in a church, workplace, or other settings. They possess skill in networking with other powerful people; they can accomplish great things.

The Star Versus Narcissistic Personality Disorder

On the continuum of personality traits, at what point do the characteristics associated with the star personality type become an unhealthy way of functioning? When good self-esteem becomes blatant selfishness on a consistent, extreme basis, the persons value themselves exclusively, above all others. Narcissistic personality disorder seriously interferes with their ability to view themselves and others realistically and to relate to other people in a healthy way. The narcissist's motto is: "I am extraordinarily and incomparably special. I am entitled to special treatment because I am superior to others." As Oldham and Morris remark, these individuals are always "looking out for number one" and the pursuit of "status, image and power" consume them.[1] The term *narcissist* originates from the name of a mythological character, Narcissus, who fell in love with his reflection in a pool and pined away for this lover whom he could not possess. While stars are ambitious and self-assured, their goal is not to avoid responsibility but to motivate others to join them in accomplishing goals. Narcissists, in contrast, have delusions of grandeur and avoid responsibility by an attitude of entitlement. While they are often charming at first impression, one may sense "coldness and ruthlessness" hidden beneath the polished exterior.[2]

While individuals with narcissistic personality disorder appear to have high self-esteem, this is actually not the case although even they may not be aware of it. In fact, they actually have poor self-esteem, and "create a huge Self in order to survive. Many of them behave (or imagine in their fantasies) as if they are the most important people in their own or the larger world, and that everyone should recognize their special place."[3] Over time they come to believe this cover-up.

Narcissistic Personality Disorder and Histrionic Personality Disorder: Similarities and Differences

The belief system of the individual with histrionic personality disorder also includes an assertion of entitlement for special treatment by others. How do the two differ on this point? Histrionics are much more subtle in their claim of "specialness." They are not blatantly arrogant, as are the narcissists. In fact, they often display a feigned helplessness and manipulate others (through the emotions of fear and guilt) into giving them special treatment based on the impression they give that they lack the ability to handle life on their own and thus need someone to take care of them. Their words and actions are carefully calculated to achieve the desired result of avoiding responsibility. On the other hand, narcissists do not appear helpless. Rather, they portray themselves as "in charge" people, incomparably competent and superior in capabilities (and often appearance) to others; thus (as they see it), they naturally deserve special treatment. Because they are so self-confident and often intimidating, narcissists frequently get the special treatment they believe they so richly deserve (especially in their dealings with more passive individuals). They give the distinct impression that others are privileged to serve them.

Another important difference between the narcissist and the histrionic is that histrionic individuals believe they must entertain others and be attractive in order to have a guarantee of having their needs met. They are "other directed." Narcissists, using others to further their own agenda, are self-directed. Millon states that they:

are independent in their orientation. That is, they turn inward for gratification, having learned to rely on themselves rather than others for safety and self-esteem. Weakness and dependency are threatening.... In sum, it is what they think of themselves, not what others say or can provide for them, that serves as the touchstone for their security and contentment. . . . [It is] the histrionic, who must perform and be attractive to win praise from others—narcissists are likely to contribute little or nothing in return for the gratifications they seek. In fact, some narcissists assume that others feel "honored" in having a relationship with them, and that others receive as much pleasure in providing them with favors and attention as the narcissist experiences in accepting these tributes.[4]

While the narcissist and the histrionic express it differently in words and actions, both personality disorders involve the faulty belief that the individual is entitled to a self-centered, "responsibility free" lifestyle at the expense of others.

Narcissistic Personality Disorder and Antisocial Personality Disorder: Similarities and Differences

Narcissistic personality disorder and antisocial personality disorder also possess similarities and differences. Millon states, "For the narcissistic type, self-esteem is based on a blind and naive assumption of personal worth and superiority. For the aggressive or antisocial type, it stems from distrust, an assumption that others will be humiliating and exploitive.... Although both passive- (narcissists) and active-independents (antisocials) devalue the standards and opinions of others, finding gratification primarily within themselves, their life histories and the strategies they employ for achieving their needs are substantially different." While the narcissist can be aggressive, the individual with antisocial personality disorder primarily takes an angry, aggressive stance with others, countering feelings of anticipated victimization with aggression.[5]

The narcissist feels entirely justified in having "special status" and often is self-assured, optimistic, and cheerful. "Narcissists experience a pervasive sense of well-being in their everyday life.... Should the balloon be burst, however, there is a rapid turn to either an edgy irritability and annoyance with others or to repeated bouts of dejection that are characterized by feeling humiliated and empty."[6]

George's Story

George is a pastor who has served in a number of churches over the past ten years. While he is a charismatic, talented individual, things don't seem to work out for him very long at any one church. He is continually frustrated that he cannot find dedicated leaders who will really commit to his ministry. George left his last church in a rage because the congregation would not agree to relocate to newer, larger facilities. He says the problem is a lack of vision and spirituality on the part of the members of the church and their lack of accepting his leadership.

While George's wife, Sarah (a quiet, reserved person), dislikes moving so frequently, she says the problem is that people just don't understand George. She says he is highly talented and believes he is the one best qualified to make the decisions at home and in the churches that he pastors. While George is known for his quick temper, Sarah states that it is because he is so intelligent that he just can't stand others' incompetency.

George, after becoming disillusioned with a particular church, quickly and easily finds a new church to pastor. The new congregational members are always attracted to his obvious talents and abilities and the way he commands respect by his self-confidence. In fact, each of the congregations has been in awe of George for the first year or so of his ministry in their respective churches, feeling fortunate to have him as their pastor. Before long, tension mounts because George must have final say on all matters. At this point, when lay leaders "challenge George's authority" (as he would state it), George resigns, citing their insubordination to the will of God.

The real problem is that George is a narcissist and does not see himself as responsible for the problems experienced in interpersonal relationships. As long as others play the role of adoring fans, often little tension is evident. However, George views disagreement as a threat since he feels entitled to a privileged position of authority and power.

Individuals with narcissistic personality disorder are truly oblivious to others' needs. When other people become assertive concerning their own needs and wants with a narcissist (who experiences delusions of grandeur), the narcissist sees this as a threat to his or her "specialness" and privileged position. The person with narcissistic personality disorder loves to associate with individuals whom he or she believes also to be "superior," to be admired by them and to be seen as their equal (yet never outshone by them, for that leads to feelings of envy in the narcissist). These individuals also feel the need to have adoring fans ("inferior" to the narcissist) in their lives (to reinforce their feelings of superiority and to do their bidding).

These individuals typically appear to be so impressive that they often experience little difficulty steamrolling others into buying into their agenda. Millon states, "It should not be surprising that the sheer presumptuousness and confidence exuded by the narcissist often elicits admiration and obedience from others."[7] While it is easy to picture a person with narcissistic personality disorder in a particular family or workplace setting, where would one typically find individuals with this type of personality disorder in the church? Most often, they are in leadership positions—for example, deacons, elders, church staff, or pastors. Persons with narcissistic personality disorder are least likely to be found in a "behind the scenes" capacity in a church, quietly and consistently doing a job. Rather, those are the individuals whom a narcissist targets for his or her own purposes.

Narcissists frequently enter the picture and take a church by storm, having left another church (or frequently a series of churches) disgruntled. During this initial honeymoon period in a new church, church members feel as if they are incredibly blessed to have these individuals because their personalities are almost irresistibly magnetic and they appear to be so talented, in their midst. Narcissists often claim to possess a special "in" with God, a "superior" form of spirituality. Members easily believe them because everything they touch seems to turn to gold (at least initially). Over time, however, the image tarnishes. They are dogmatic and intolerant of others, and when those with narcissistic personality disorder do not get their way, they reveal their quick temper (which they consider righteous indignation).

Frequently, church members who have been godly, faithful workers over a number of years leave the church, if the narcissist does not leave, because of the pain the narcissist has inflicted by a harsh, superior, and judgmental attitude. Many church splits have occurred involving a person with narcissistic personality disorder, frequently leaving members spiritually and emotionally wounded.

Criteria for Narcissistic Personality Disorder

The criteria for Narcissistic Personality Disorder as listed in the DSM-IV are as follows:

A pervasive pattern of grandiosity (in fantasy or behavior), need for admiration, and lack of empathy, beginning by early adulthood and present in a variety of contexts, as indicated by five (or more) of the following:

1. has a grandiose sense of self-importance (e.g., exaggerates achievements and talents, expects to be recognized as superior without commensurate achievements)
2. is preoccupied with fantasies of unlimited success, power, brilliance, beauty, or ideal love
3. believes that he or she is "special" and unique and can only be understood by, or should associate with, other special or

high-status people (or institutions)
4. requires excessive admiration
5. has a sense of entitlement, i.e., unreasonable expectations of especially favorable treatment or automatic compliance with his or her expectations
6. is interpersonally exploitative, i.e., takes advantage of others to achieve his or her own ends
7. lacks empathy; is unwilling to recognize or identify with the feelings and needs of others
8. is often envious of others or believes that others are envious of him or her
9. shows arrogant, haughty behaviors or attitudes[8]

Belief System of Individuals with Narcissistic Personality Disorder

What do narcissists believe about themselves and others? Their belief system is summarized as follows:

1. I am a very special person.
2. Since I am so superior, I am entitled to special treatment and privileges.
3. I don't have to be bound by the rules that apply to other people.
4. It is very important to get recognition, praise, and admiration.
5. If others don't respect my status, they should be punished.
6. Other people should satisfy my needs.
7. Other people should recognize how special I am.
8. It's intolerable if I'm not accorded my due respect or don't get what I'm entitled to.
9. Other people don't deserve the admiration or riches that they have.
10. People have no right to criticize me.
11. No one's needs should interfere with my own.
12. Since I am so talented, people should go out of their way to promote my career.
13. Only people as brilliant as I am understand me.
14. I have every reason to expect grand things.[9]

These beliefs epitomize arrogance and seem almost unbelievable to those of us who have lived our lives trying to consider and respect the needs of others as we attempt to follow the Golden Rule. However, individuals with narcissistic personality disorder operate by a different set of rules and are often able to continue in a pattern of entitlement with remarkable ease, for others are typically, at least initially, in awe of their "larger than life" presence.

Feelings Experienced by Others

Feelings often are the alarm system for detecting the presence of a personality disorder. What feelings do others typically experience when they associate with a person with narcissistic personality disorder? Frequently, a feeling of inferiority to these individuals is a first reaction. Many feel intimidated by their polished appearance and self-confident demeanor. Initially, people can feel flattered to be the object of these individuals' attention and try to please them to keep their attention.

In contrast to the feeling of being drawn to these individuals, another common experience is feeling threatened by and in competition with them. Because they present themselves as superior, individuals may feel in danger of being replaced by others with whom the narcissist has contact. Others may also feel incompetent compared to these individuals (for example, in the workplace or in a church). Therefore, feeling threatened, competitive, and resentful toward the individual is common.

The competitive nature of the narcissist often occurs in a marital relationship. Narcissists often marry mates they feel have "special" characteristics only to become competitive with their spouses when they get more attention than the narcissist. "They want to be married to someone special, but they become angry when they lose the spotlight."[10]

When one is in a relationship with a person with narcissistic personality disorder, over time a feeling of being manipulated is common. While the narcissist is openly arrogant and not typically sneaky like the person with histrionic personality disorder (manipulation being the primary mode of operation for the histrionic), the narcissist, if not able to achieve what he or she desires by other means, will resort to using manipulation. This manipulation often involves making others feel "less than" the narcissist and trying to "con" other persons into feeling that they can't live without the "superior" individual by their side. Narcissists must be admired by others at all times. When this does not occur, "they are consumed with feelings of envy and rage and disdain for others; they grow depressed and find little satisfaction or contentment from their work or from the people in their lives."[11]

In the presence of a person with narcissistic personality disorder, do others experience increased or decreased feelings of self-esteem? While people may feel special due to the attention received from a narcissist, they also feel inferior to the individual. Thus, they are placed in a double bind (purposely) by the narcissist. If narcissists can succeed in making an individual feel important, a good feeling, and at the same time inferior to them, the person is indeed emotionally vulnerable. This can lead to a person's feeling trapped, dependent on the narcissist for the prestige that he or she brings and yet consistently being cast in the role of a second-string player in life.

Others may experience a love/hate relationship with the narcissist. "They are simultaneously taken in by charm and exploited in some way. Narcissists are apt to become most resentful and contemptuous of anyone who tries to hold them accountable for their exploitative, self-centered behavior."[12] When the charm of the narcissist wears thin, others may feel rage against the individual, for through their entitled attitude toward life, they seem to be given everything others must earn through discipline and hard work.

Factors in the Development of Narcissistic Personality Disorder: Nature Versus Nurture

What causes an individual to develop narcissistic personality disorder? Is it nature or nurture? Millon states that no clear evidence indicates a biological component to the development of narcissistic personality disorder; rather the environment is a major contributing factor in creating narcissistic personality disorder, for this is where one finds "the roots of the pattern."[13]

Home Environment

What type of environment could create or foster this disorder? Among differing opinions, two theories are offered from the perspectives of Kernberg and Millon. Kernberg maintains that narcissistic personality disorder involves cold, distant parents who reject the child. However, ironically, discovery of a talent or ability places the child in a special role, which the child must maintain in order to keep the parent's approval.[14] "This quality of specialness serves as a refuge, at first only temporarily but ultimately an often-returned-to haven that reliably offsets the underlying feeling of having been unloved by the vengefully rejecting parent."[15]

Millon's theory of the development of narcissistic personality disorder, however, is different from Kernberg's. Millon sees it emerging from a family background in which "some parents come to view their child as 'God's gift to mankind.' These parents pamper and indulge their youngsters in ways that teach them that their every wish is a command, that they can receive without giving in return, and that they deserve prominence without even minimal effort."[16]

This can be viewed as a form of abuse referred to as "empowering abuse." More familiar is a type of abuse termed "disempowering abuse," which involves physical and emotional abuse occurring when a child is not valued for who he or she is as a person, judging the child to be inferior in some way. In empowering abuse children are made to feel superior.[17] They are not bound by the same rules others are expected to follow; they develop a "little prince" or "little princess" mentality. They are taught that this superiority entitles them to be self-centered, ignoring others' needs. Empowering abuse can be subtle, and parents may believe they are teaching their child to be self-confident, self-assured individuals. However, the implications for children who experience this type of abuse as they grow into adulthood is enormous.

"The result of empowering experiences is that children grow up to become offenders or victimizers . . . the children who get empowered, and never disempowered, are often in a difficult position in that they are 'self will run riot,' controlling people by abusive behavior that gets out of control. They often are very offensive and may believe they are entitled to take from others and use others."[18] Narcissistic personality disorder can emerge from the experience of empowering abuse.

While disempowering abuse feels bad, empowering abuse can actually feel good, nevertheless being harmful to the individual in the long run. While growing up, although this sense of superiority may generate poor relationships with others who do not share their opinion, these individuals may be deluded into thinking all is right with their world as they lead a privileged and entitled lifestyle. However, "teaching people that they are superior to others is erroneous and dysfunctional" and leads to abusive relationships, causing much pain.[19]

While overindulgent parents who foster a sense of superiority in their children may believe they are giving their child everything they did not have as children (including a high degree of self-esteem), this style of parenting can result in dysfunctional behavior. These parents are actually fostering a pseudo-self-esteem based on a distortion of the truth.

Many believe that parents who are afraid to set healthy limits for their children and who provide them with an overabundance of material possessions set these children up for failure later in life. These self-centered individuals do not adequately develop the necessary work ethic and skills to contribute to society and, therefore, become exclusively "takers" in life. This sense of entitlement without regard for others is a primary difference between the star and the individual with narcissistic personality disorder. The star is self-assured, ambitious, and good at motivating others to join in accomplishing great things. In contrast, individuals with narcissistic personality disorder in their arrogance exploit others and feel little need to contribute to society.

Hope and Help: The Story of the Woman at the Well

Can a narcissist change? As we see from the biblical story of the woman at the well, an individual with the traits of narcissistic personality disorder can indeed change when he or she has been transformed by a genuine relationship with God. In John 4, we read the narrative in which Jesus spoke with the woman at the well. As Samaritans and Jews did not commonly associate with one another, this Samaritan woman was surprised when Jesus spoke to her and requested a drink of water. There are hints that lead us to believe that this woman possessed personality traits indicative of a narcissist. For example, she flaunted her religious heritage when speaking with Jesus (John 4:19—20), implying that Samaritan forefathers were superior to the Jews. She showed evidence of an attitude of entitlement, without any remorse. She had relationships with a number of men, there being no indication that any of her husbands had died. Rather, she was probably divorced from a number of men or was simply living with a series of men. She does not follow the pattern of a dependent personality; rather, she appeared to believe that others existed for her use.

Encountering Jesus, however, changed her life. Confronted about her past, she acknowledged Jesus as a prophet and responded to the forgiveness Christ offered. Repentant, she was eager to share the good news of forgiveness. With the characteristic charisma of a narcissist, she rushed to tell others about Jesus and attracted a number of listeners. Many Samaritans became believers in Jesus because of her testimony and having heard the words of Jesus for themselves. She demonstrated what is needed in the life of the narcissist, embracing the unconditional love of Jesus and showing goodness and true empathy for others in sharing the good news that she received.

Spiritual Needs of the Narcissist: Fruit of the Spirit—Goodness

Narcissists need to experience the unconditional love of God for behind the facade of superiority, at the core of their being is a lack of self-esteem, which they are vehement in hiding to the point they choose not to acknowledge this lack even to themselves. God's love is the great equalizer of human beings in that it is given equally to all without strings attached; and concurrently, God's love elevates the human experience to a higher level, that of a birthright as children of God, heirs with Christ.

Narcissists also need to develop the fruit of the spirit that they are lacking, that of goodness. Self-consumed, they do not consider the needs of others. Developing goodness allows them to care about and empathize with others; in doing so they become the authentic, loving people they were created to be. This is not an easy process for narcissists; yet with God's help and others' support, they can become great people of integrity. Change involves a spirit of true repentance, as we saw with the woman at the well. The selfishness, which has eclipsed the strength of their personality (magnetic, charismatic), is replaced by a loving, empathetic spirit, and they are freed to live a life of authenticity in which God's love can shine through them.

Change is possible for the narcissist. Typically, however, a narcissist is not motivated to change their attitudes or actions unless they experience great loss.

> Narcissists typically size up those around them and quickly train those who are so disposed to honor them; for example, narcissists frequently select a dependent mate who will be obeisant, solicitous, and subservient, without expecting anything in return except strength and assurances of fidelity. It is central to narcissists' interpersonal style that good fortune will come to them without reciprocity. Since they feel entitled to get what they wish and have been successful in having others provide them with comforts they have not deserved, narcissists have little reason to discontinue their habitual presumptuous and exploitive behaviors.[20]

This is similar to histrionic personality disorder. Rather than do the hard work of changing in order to become authentic and responsible, both histrionics and narcissists commonly find others who will take care of their needs. Only when they run out of fans will they feel any motivation to make necessary changes in their lives, or, in the case of the narcissists, if the discrepancy between their actual abilities and their grandiose sense of capability becomes unmanageable. Commonly, if they enter therapy, it is because they are depressed or anxious over the loss of a significant person in their lives (whom they feel they can't replace) or, for narcissists, if they have suffered humiliation in the eyes of the public due to their level of performance. As Millon states, "The inexhaustible reservoir of self-faith of narcissists can withstand considerable draining before it runs dry."[21]

When narcissists enter therapy, they are often looking for a "quick fix" to restore their feelings of control and self-confidence. Rather than desiring to develop a life of integrity, making a meaningful contribution to society and serving others, their goals are exclusively self-serving in nature. Because they believe admitting to shortcomings shows weakness, something they must avoid at all costs, they are frequently hostile and demanding of therapists (and others who try to help them in the process of change). "Great patience and equanimity are required to establish a spirit of genuine confidence and respect."[22]

How to Help

Here are some suggestions for dealing with an individual with narcissistic personality disorder:

1. Be aware that narcissists can become violent. Kennedy and Charles state that narcissists can react in extreme ways to the experience of loss. They remark, "Their sense of grandiosity and entitlement, coupled with their seeming inability to feel empathy for others, make them difficult to work with and, in certain circumstances, dangerous to others.... Their rage can be literally murderous in nature."[23] Do not underestimate the possibility of violence on the part of the narcissist when he or she has experienced loss or threat of loss or has been confronted by others regarding his or her behavior.

2. Be alert to feelings of flattery, inferiority, competition, and threat, which these individuals produce in others. Actions, not words, tell the story. Look at their past relationships to determine if they follow a "fight or flight" pattern when they are held accountable for actions. As Kennedy and Charles aptly state regarding contact with a narcissist, "The first concern for nonprofessionals is to avoid being incorporated into their psychological maneuvering."[24]

3. Show genuine appreciation for their starlike qualities of drawing others to themselves and showing leadership capabilities. However, set clear expectations and limits on their behavior, including giving them only their fair share of your time and attention. Reinforce boundaries with action. "Patience, persistence, and confidence in setting appropriate limits will probably prove to be important allies" when dealing with a narcissist.[25]

4. Give them the opportunity and encouragement to develop talents in a safe, nonthreatening environment. Often narcissists circumvent usual ways of achieving—for example, further education—because they believe that if they fail they can no longer assert their superiority. "Narcissists assume that the presumption of superiority will suffice as

its proof. ... Many narcissists begin to recognize in time that they cannot 'live up' to their self-made publicity and fear trying themselves out in the real world. ... As a consequence, however, narcissists paralyze themselves. Their unfounded sense of confidence and their omnipotent belief in their perfection inhibit them from developing whatever aptitudes they may in fact possess."[26]

5. Be aware that the narcissist responds best when initially working on short-term goals, which he or she finds meaningful. However, to address these issues without helping them change their attitudes toward themselves and others, primarily regarding "the three major components of narcissism: grandiosity, hypersensitivity to evaluation, and lack of empathy" is doing them a disservice.[27] This is usually beyond the scope of a friend, coworker, or pastor. Don't hesitate to refer the individual for counseling.

6. Be realistic about what the narcissist is typically capable of giving to others. Dependence on narcissists for one's own well-being and self-esteem sets one up for great disappointment, for they have not developed the character traits of empathy and sacrificial love for others. Others tend to blame themselves when they are in a floundering or failed relationship with a narcissist because the narcissist takes no responsibility and often convincingly blames the other person for the failure of the relationship. If you are in this position, participate in counseling so that you can see a more realistic view of the situation and learn to stop blaming yourself. Supportive friends are crucial to your emotional health. Remember that the narcissist can become violent. If you could be in danger, seek help immediately.

7. Expect to have difficulty feeling compassion for them. However, while in no way excusing their behavior or allowing oneself to be emotionally vulnerable to them, the most merciful view of their situation involves the realization that they were created to be the way they are by the experience of abuse, empowering abuse that limits their potential as human beings for forming truly caring and loving relationships. While it is often infuriating when they appear to have received the "goodies" in life without having earned them, theirs is a shallow existence and not really to be envied, for they are incapable of experiencing genuine, deep, and abiding love for themselves and others which is, after all, the greatest of joys.

◆ Five ◆

The Lonesome Dove and Avoidant Personality Disorder

*I*f the lonesome dove type could work up the courage, he or she could market an appealing ad in the personal section of the newspaper. Available: Dating Partner who is sensitive to the needs of others, faithful, gentle, loveable, and unassuming; a "till death do us part" kind of person.

Oldham and Morris identify six traits of this "Sensitive Personality":

1. These individuals are most comfortable with the familiar and the routine.
2. They are very much concerned about what others think of them.
3. The sensitive type is careful about the way he or she relates to others.
4. They are courteous and self-disciplined in their demeanor.
5. They function best in situations that are structured and in which expectations are clear.
6. Sensitive people are reticent to share their intimate thoughts with others.[1]

The novel *Lonesome Dove* by Larry McMurtry was such a best-seller that it was turned into a miniseries for television. The film's enormous popularity stemmed in large part from the faithful, feisty relationship that existed between the two main characters of the story—Woodrow Call and Gus McCrae. As the novel begins, these two retired Texas Rangers have settled down in Lonesome Dove, South Texas—a sleepy, basically safe town—far away from robbers and the Indian Wars of the 1870s that once absorbed their attention. As the story progresses, it becomes clear that Lonesome Dove is more than the name of the town; it is a symbol of Captain Call's personality (played by Tommy Lee Jones; Robert Duvall is cast as Augustus McCrae). Almost all of the characteristics of the sensitive type or, as we label it—lonesome dove, fit Call.

1. Captain Call was most comfortable with the familiar and the routine. Our hero in the novel lived out in the open land, the contours of which never changed. Call also knew the weather well, with its predictable seasons, and he had learned to adjust his life to them. Captain Call was also a lover of animals, especially horses. He had broken and ridden them for years, and now, along with his newly acquired herd of cattle, he and McCrae and their hired hands planned to move to Montana to try their luck at ranching there. Moreover, as the story progresses, it becomes clear that the captain was comfortable with only two people—Gus and Newt (Call's son by Maggie, a prostitute, but who was never told he was the Captain's boy).

2. Related to the first characteristic, Woodrow Call functioned best in situations that were structured and in which expectations were clear. He learned to appreciate regimentation as a captain in the Texas Rangers, and, now, as a cattle owner, leading a group of men three thousand miles from Lonesome Dove, Texas, to Montana, he expected order and obedience from his workers. On the journey the captain executed one of his workers (Jake) because he became a horse thief.

3. Captain Call was careful how he related to others. His words were few but dependable. He never married the love of his life (Maggie, who died ten years before the story began), nor did he ever tell Newt that he was his father. The main character in the story kept pretty much to himself, keeping company with only a handful of people at best.

4. Nevertheless, the captain was courteous and self-disciplined in demeanor. He took his hat off in the presence of women and bowed his head at the funeral of a friend. Two incidents in the film especially

convey Call's courtesy. The first (an ironic display of courtesy) was when an army scout tried to take Call's horses by conscription. In the heated discussion that ensued, the scout hit Newt for refusing to surrender his mount to the army. At that point, Captain Call whipped the scout soundly. When Call walked away from the defeated soldier, he was heard to say, "I hate rude behavior in a man!" The second incident, a sad one, occurred at the end of the movie, when Gus's love, Clara, expressed her distaste for Call's coming between her and Gus. "If it weren't for you," Clara yelled, "Gus would have married me!" But rather than talk back to her, Call quietly, gently walked away without an argument.

5. Call's dominant trait was his reticence to share his intimate thoughts with others, even the two dearest people in his life—Gus and Newt. The captain could show care for his fellow Texas Ranger only by teasing him. At the end of the story, Call could not muster the courage to express his deep feelings for Gus. In a memorable scene, after taking Gus' body from Montana back to Texas (before Gus died from gangrene in his legs as a result of being hit by arrows from marauding Indians, he made Call promise that he would bury him back in Texas), standing over his newly dug grave, Call muttered, "There, this will teach me to be more careful about what I promise." At the end of the story, Call still could not bring himself to tell Newt that he was his son.

The lonesome dove personality type can make a positive impression on others and, given time, endear themselves to people. But that is just the problem, for the sensitive type has great difficulty warming up to others. In fact, if left alone, such individuals are capable of becoming recluses. If lonesome doves fail to develop close friends, their propensity to anxiety, struggle with poor self-esteem and social ineptness can become emotionally debilitating. When that happens, the lonesome dove type has transitioned into avoidant personality disorder. People who exist at that end of the personality continuum feel different from others and perceive themselves as left out. They tend to be self-conscious and inarticulate. Perhaps the most distressing dynamic driving individuals with avoidant personality is the painful paradox of deeply desiring friendship and companionship with others while anxiously dreading that people will truly get to know them and not like what they find. Rather than run the risk of personal rejection, the overly sensitive type avoids the presence of that which they need the most—people.

Avoidant Personality Disorder

The term avoidant personality was first used by Millon.[2] He described this personality as consisting of an "active-detached" pattern representing "a fear and mistrust of others." He writes: "These individuals maintain a constant vigil lest their impulses and longing for affection result in a repetition of the pain and anguish they have experienced with others previously. Only by active withdrawal can they protect themselves. Despite desires to relate, they have learned it is best to deny these feelings and keep an interpersonal distance."[3]

Burnham, Gladstone, and Gibson relate avoidant persons to the "need-fear dilemma":

> He has an inordinate need for external structure and control.... [His] existence depends upon his maintaining contact with objects.... The very excessiveness of his need for objects also makes them inordinately dangerous and fearsome since they can destroy him through abandonment. Hence, he fears and distrusts them.
>
> [One way] to avert or alleviate the pain of his need-fear dilemma [is] ... object avoidance ....
>
> Attempts by others to engage him in interaction are regarded as intrusions which carry the threat of disorganization.[4]

Horney anticipated Millon with his description of the plight of an "interpersonally avoidant" person: "On little or no provocation he feels that others look down on him, do not take him seriously, do not care for his company, and, in fact, slight him. His self-contempt... make[s] him... profoundly uncertain about the attitudes of others toward him. Being unable to accept himself as he is, he cannot possibly believe that others, knowing him with all his shortcomings, can accept him in a friendly or appreciative spirit."[5]

Sally's Story: Portrait of a Wallflower

Meet Sally. You could not find a more endearing person. Here was a dependable, gentle, diligent individual who was a model wife, mother, and employee. She was faithful to her husband all of their marriage. Her children grew up to call her blessed. Her job of thirty years rewarded her capable, persistent service with award after award. Yet whenever Sally was expected to attend a social gathering in connection with her job or family or on those rare occasions when she invited neighbors to her home or even to attend church, She seemed to unravel. Her stomach churned, her mouth became dry, and words failed her. This condition extended back into Sally's youth. Even as a teenager she struggled to make friends and found dating difficult. And when Sally did work up the courage to attend a dance, she accepted her self-imposed role of being the proverbial wallflower. She felt uninteresting, clumsy, and even ugly.

Sally's frame of mind did not improve with the passing of time. She eventually married, but her marriage to an alcoholic made for a difficult relationship, not to mention causing havoc with her social life. Sally did not cultivate friendships with significant others (except for her two children and two sisters). Before attending social gatherings or work-related group meetings, Sally felt exhausted and looked for reasons not to attend the event. When she did show up, she was inarticulate, failed to make eye contact with people, and generally stayed quiet. Believing she would make a fool of herself during those seemingly endless moments, Sally remained silent.

Back at home Sally brooded over not being socially adept and having more friends. She lamented her apparent inferiority, feeling anxious, lonely, and sad. Sally's marriage to an alcoholic exacerbated the problem. On numerous occasions her husband's inebriated behavior at family outings humiliated her to the point of tears. Often she would find another ride home so as not to expose herself to the shame of it all. Consequently, Sally was hesitant to invite even her few friends into her home for fear they would see her husband in a drunken stupor. She belonged to no organizations, rarely attended church, and generally kept to herself. In short, Sally was shame ridden.

This portrait fits avoidant personality disorder. Sally's alarm at the thought of close contact with others and reticence to be transparent in social settings paradoxically created, and yet revealed, the source of her problem. Sally desperately needed that which she avoided the most—people. On the one hand, she deeply longed for meaningful relationships while, on the other hand, Sally feared people would reject her. Consequently, her life was characterized by loneliness, anxiety, and sadness.

The DSM-IV describes avoidant personality disorder as:

> A pervasive pattern of social inhibition, feelings of inadequacy, and hypersensitivity to negative evaluation beginning by early adulthood and present in a variety of contexts, as indicated by four (or more) of the following:

1. avoids occupational activities that involve significant interpersonal contact, because of fears of criticism, disapproval, or rejection
2. is unwilling to get involved with people unless certain of being liked
3. shows restraint within intimate relationships because of the fear of being ashamed or ridiculed
4. is preoccupied with being criticized or rejected in social situations
5. is inhibited in new interpersonal situations because of feelings of inadequacy
6. views self as socially inept, personally unappealing, or inferior to others
7. is unusually reluctant to take personal risks or to engage in any new activities because they may prove embarrassing[6]

The belief system of the individual with avoidant personality disorder includes:

1. I am socially inept and socially undesirable in work or social situations.
2. Other people are potentially critical, indifferent, demeaning, or rejecting.
3. I cannot tolerate unpleasant feelings.
4. If people get close to me, they will discover the "real" me and reject me.
5. Being exposed as inferior or inadequate will be intolerable.
6. I should avoid unpleasant situations at all costs.
7. If I feel or think something unpleasant, I should try to wipe it out or distract myself—for example, think of something else, have a drink, take a drug, or watch television.
8. I should avoid situations in which I attract attention, or I should be as inconspicuous as possible.
9. Unpleasant feelings will escalate and get out of control.
10. If others criticize me, they must be right.
11. It is better not to do anything than to try something that might fail.
12. If I don't think about a problem, I don't have to do anything about it.
13. Signs of tension in a relationship indicate the relationship has gone bad; therefore, I should cut it off.
14. If I ignore a problem, it will go away.[7]

In addition to social evasion, those with avoidant personality disorder demonstrate attitudinal or cognitive avoidance in that they subconsciously shun dysphoria—feelings of discomfort. Sadness, anxiety, loneliness, anger, or bad moods are not permissible for avoidant individuals. Their fear is that if they allow themselves to feel such dysphoria, it will get out of hand, and this will reflect badly on them. To prevent feeling bad, avoidants unknowingly engage in behavior designed to detract them from uncomfortable emotions.

> Avoidant patients become aware of a dysphoric feeling. (They may or may not be fully aware of the thoughts that precede or accompany the emotion.) Their tolerance for the dysphoria is low, so they take a "fix" to distract themselves and make them feel better. They may discontinue a task or fail to initiate a task they had planned to do. They may turn on the television, pick up something to read, reach for food or a cigarette, get up and walk around, and so forth. In short, they seek a diversion in order to push the uncomfortable thoughts out of mind. This pattern of cognitive and behavioral avoidance, having been reinforced by a reduction of dysphoria, eventually becomes ingrained and automatic.[8]

Although avoidants deeply desire to cultivate long-term, meaningful relationships, the price of reaching that goal—transparency and tension—is too high for them. Instead, the overly sensitive individual looks to the fictitious future—that right person or the perfect job will come along—for deliverance. Consequently, avoidants look outside themselves to find solutions to their problems. But what they really need is to realize that by being honest in expressing their feelings with others, despite ensuing tension, is the key to developing friendships. In pursuing that path, sensitive individuals need not look elsewhere for ideal partners and colleagues.

Jack, who suffers from avoidant personality disorder, is outwardly always positive and cheerful at his job. Once, while combing his hair in the bathroom, his boss casually remarked to him that he appreciated Jack's friendly disposition. "In fact," Jack's employer said, "I don't remember ever seeing you when you weren't happy and positive." But what apparently was Jack's strength, in actuality was his weakness. Because Jack feared others would reject him if he displayed any negative emotions, he put on a front. The truth of the matter was that Jack had been dissatisfied with his job for the ten or so years he had worked there. Others would have been shocked to discover that

Jack prayed daily for God to provide him the "right" job so that he could feel a part of, and at home with, his colleagues at work. Yet what Jack needed was to learn to get in touch with his feelings, both positive and negative, and then have the courage to share them with others. In doing that, Jack would be surprised to learn that his fellow workers, who in fact cared deeply for him, would be undaunted by his negative emotions and would accept him all the more. This, in turn, would liberate Jack to be himself and, consequently, to enjoy his present job.

Emotions Generated by Avoidants

What type of feelings do such individuals generate in others? Three reactions quickly come to mind. First, those in the presence of someone with avoidant personality disorder experience a sense of being uncomfortable because the avoidant person has difficulty maintaining eye contact due to shyness and sheepishness. This creates uneasiness in others. Second, avoidants communicate confusion to those with whom they speak. This is the result of the mixed messages avoidants send. On the one hand, the overly sensitive person's desire to fellowship with people signals warmth, while, on the other hand, his or her social reticence signals interpersonal distance. Such a message mirrors the core problem of the sensitive type, namely, they desire that which they avoid—people. Third, besides uneasiness and confusion, avoidants unintentionally can also make others feel guilty. Shyness and lack of eye contact can easily be misinterpreted by their conversation partners as indicating that something is wrong with them or, perhaps, they think they have said or done something to the avoidant that was hurtful.

These feelings of discomfort, confusion, and even guilt that avoidants generate in others are intensified when the sensitive type attempts to converse with a person of a different race or gender. Furthermore, avoidants give false signals to people when, because of the embarrassment of not knowing, they pretend to understand what another person is saying even if they do not comprehend it. To admit not grasping what is being communicated to them is difficult for avoidants because it makes them feel stupid. This makes the educational process, in general, a formidable obstacle to the sensitive individual.

Causes of Avoidant Personality Disorder

What causes avoidant personality disorder? Two factors are usually identified in the scholarly literature: nature and nurture. Typically the avoidant pattern begins early in life, resulting in part from innate biological factors.[9] Socially timid children at the early age of two already display heightened sensitivity to various types of environmental change, including fluctuating social conditions.[10] But biological predisposition alone is insufficient to account for the emergence of this condition. Environmental factors deepened social timidity into the long-standing behavior characterizing the avoidant individual. Consider the negative influence driving the disorder.

As children, they may have had a significant person (parent, sibling, peer) who was highly critical and rejecting of them. They developed certain schemas from interactions with that person, such as "I'm inadequate," "I'm defective," "I'm unlikable," "I'm different," "I don't fit in." They also developed schemas about other people: "People don't care about me," "People will reject me." Not all children with critical, rejecting significant others, however, become avoidant. Avoidant patients must make certain assumptions to explain the negative interactions: "I must be a bad person for my mother to treat me so badly," "I must be different or defective—that's why I have no friends," "If my parents don't like me, how could anyone?" As children, and later as adults, avoidant patients make the error of assuming that others will react to them in the same negative fashion as the critical significant person did. They continually fear that others will find them lacking and will reject them. They are afraid they won't be able to bear the dysphoria that they believe will arise from the rejection. So they avoid social situations and relationships, sometimes severely limiting their lives, to avoid the pain they expect to feel when someone inevitably (in their judgment) rejects them.[11]

Several studies indicate that avoidant personality disorder is distinguished from other conditions with similar features, such as social phobias,[12] schizoid personality disorder,[13] and dependent personality disorder.[14] Concerning the first of these, while social phobics avoid certain public circumstances (for example, public speaking or large parties), they do not shy away from close relationships as avoidants do. Regarding schizoid individuals, although they, like avoidants, shun close relationships, unlike avoidants, schizoid persons have no desire for intimate friends, nor do they care when they are criticized by others. Although avoidants resemble dependents in manifesting low self-esteem, avoidants neither rely on others for decision-making nor do they subordinate their needs in order to ensure that a relationship will continue.

Treatment of the Condition

Treatment of avoidant personality disorder is difficult to implement because the condition itself deters individuals from engaging in long-term therapy. Yet two techniques used by therapists have met with measured success: exposure strategies and group therapy. The first involves teaching verbal communication skills through graduated social experiences, moving from easier situations to more difficult ones (for example, conversing with an acquaintance at work, expressing satisfaction with one's achievements, voicing fears to a friend). The second strategy, group therapy, helps to alleviate the avoidant's sense of distance from others. Hearing about others' anxieties with the same condition reduces isolation.[15]

Moses, the Shy One

Do people of faith suffer from avoidant personality disorder? Yes, they do—because they are human and because they live in a fallen world. Take Moses, for example. The Bible describes that great deliverer of ancient Jews as the "meekest man in all the earth" (Num. 12:3). Using our term, he was a "lonesome dove." Moses was also susceptible to avoidant personality disorder. The cause for that condition began in Moses' childhood. He was born a Hebrew slave to the ancient Egyptians. And even though God divinely orchestrated his deliverance and subsequent rearing in Pharaoh's court (Exod. 2:1−10), surely the shame of being a servant silently but significantly shaped the core of Moses' life. The pain of it all came to the fore when, after killing the Egyptian who was harming a fellow Jew, another Jew sent Moses fleeing into the desert by ridiculing him as God's supposed deliverer (Exod. 2:11−15), not to mention introducing in him fear for his life. For many years thereafter shame and anxiety dominated Moses' existence, banishing him to obscurity.

Note how the seven traits of avoidant personality disorder fit Moses. First, he was easily hurt by criticism or disapproval. Thus, the grumblings against God and Moses by the wilderness generation deeply offended him (Num. 16:41−42). Second, there is no record that Moses cultivated intimate friendships. Social distance even affected his relationship with his brother

Aaron and sister Miriam (Num. 12). And perhaps a part of Moses' rationale for delegating leadership of the Jews to seventy elders stemmed from his inability to get close to his people (Exod. 18). Third, Moses was unwilling to get involved with his compatriots for fear they would reject him (Exod. 4:1–2). Fourth and fifth, Moses' avoidance of interpersonal interaction and his fear of speaking inappropriately are evident in the way he hunted for excuses not to be God's spokesman to Pharaoh on behalf of the Jews (Exod. 4:10–13). Sixth, there is also indication that Moses, like overly sensitive people, was afraid of showing his emotions to others. Judging from Exodus 34:33–35 and the subsequent commentary of 2 Corinthians 3:12–13, Moses seems to have continued to wear a veil to disguise the diminishing glory of God on his face. Was Moses embarrassed by his weakness? Seventh, avoidant individuals exaggerate the difficulties, dangers, and risks involved in doing something ordinary but outside their routine. Stated another way, avoidants seek structure to capture a sense of security. Is that why, among other reasons, Moses promulgated 613 laws?

Is there help for those who struggle because they have avoidant personality disorder? Most definitely. Group therapy and gradual exposure to social settings provide relief for those afflicted with this condition. From a spiritual point of view, the fruit of joy (Gal. 5:22) is what avoidants need. The key to this is helping them realize that God through Christ accepts them unconditionally and, therefore, will never chide or embarrass them. Furthermore, a loving, nurturing church can reinforce this truth to avoidants that they will never be rejected. In the environment of a friendly and faithful congregation, lonesome doves can grow in security, develop relationships, and dedicate their gifts to God and for good. In time the shame and anxiety that characterizes avoidants can be demonstrated to be without basis in fact, and the joy of the Spirit can liberate them.

Let us return to the illustration in our introduction about John, lonesome dove. John, through the joy of divine acceptance and the encouragement of the people of God, experienced significant help to cope with his avoidant personality disorder. He effectively dealt with the seven signs of that condition. In doing so, his example provides some practical suggestions for those in a similar situation.

1. Now that John has come to realize that God and his church accept him for who he is, he is better equipped to handle criticism. When it comes, John no longer feels rejected. If the critique is valid, he learns from it; when it is not, he dismisses it.

2. Because of John's affiliation with the church, he has developed a number of close friends, especially older gentlemen who serve as godly mentors for him.

3. Because John has been involved in his church's outreach, he has learned to reach out to people outside the faith, even if they respond negatively to him.

4. John's growth in the Spirit, and with the help of the people of God, has empowered him to meet and interact with people, as well as to spread his wings and fly in terms of using his spiritual gifts in the service of others.

5. Rather than being intimidated by social tasks such as public speaking, John now regularly shares spiritual truths before his congregation.

6. Little by little John has become more transparent in sharing his feelings with others. Consequently, the Spirit and the people of God have brought him comfort as he has wept and revealed his fears to others.

7. John has been able to balance out his need for structure and organization with spontaneity, joy, and freedom in the Spirit.

Conclusion

This chapter has been devoted to a discussion of avoidant personality disorder, its description, causes, symptoms, belief system, and treatment. Along the way we have noted illustrations of the overly sensitive type in day-to-day life and in the Bible, as well as focused on the fruit of joy that is needed to address the struggles associated with that condition. The goal in all of this is to diminish the weaknesses of avoidant personality disorder so that the strengths of the lonesome dove type can become visible: sensitive to the needs of others, faithful, gentle, loving, and capable. And even when the struggle of avoidant personality disorder persists, such an individual can find comfort in the truth that God, who has created and redeemed us, perfects his power through our weakness (2 Cor. 12:9).

◆ Six ◆

The Sentinel and Paranoid Personality Disorder

What do Rush Limbaugh, Jesse Jackson, and Ralph Nader have in common? All are sentinels for their respective causes. Their motto could well be, "Eternal vigilance is the price of freedom." The sentinel personality type is a good person to have on your side. Their independent thinking, savvy in sizing up people and situations, and alertness to pending danger make them champions of the oppressed or even the slighted. They often pose a formidable obstacle to those who would abuse the rights of others.

But vigilance can be taken too far. When that occurs, the sentinel moves toward the other side of the continuum, a condition known as paranoid personality disorder. Such people are "apprehensive, suspicious, uncompromising, and argumentative, and they're convinced of their rightness beyond the shadow of a doubt. Individuals with paranoid personality disorder are on guard against a hostile universe, where bad things happen or are always about to happen to them at the hands of other people."[1] This maladaptive perspective is the driving force behind doomsday prophets, militia groups, and conspiracy theorists. Like Chicken Little, their message is alarming: "the sky is falling, the sky is falling." Thus a pastor warned his church of the disasters predicted that would accompany Y2K (when some computers will be unable to register the year 2000). He urged his people to exchange their cash for gold, stock up on food, and buy a gun! What the person suffering from paranoid personality disorder needs to realize is that the other guy is not always the enemy. This truth is vividly illustrated in the story told by Frank Koch in *Proceedings*, the magazine of the Naval Institute:

> Two battleships assigned to the training squadron had been at sea on maneuvers in heavy weather for several days. I was serving on the lead battleship and was on watch on the bridge as night fell. The visibility was poor with patchy fog, so the captain remained on the bridge keeping an eye on all activities. Shortly after dark, the lookout on the wing of the bridge reported, "Light, bearing on the starboard bow." "Is it steady or moving astern?" the captain called out. Lookout replied, "Steady, captain," which meant we were on a dangerous collision course with that ship. The captain then called to the signalman, "Signal that ship: We are on a collision course, advise you change course 20 degrees." Back came a signal, "Advisable for you to change course 20 degrees." The captain said, "Send, I'm a captain, change course 20 degrees." "I'm a seaman second class," came the reply. "You had better change course 20 degrees." By that time, the captain was furious. He spat out, "Send, I'm a battleship. Change course 20 degrees." Back came the flashing light, "I'm a lighthouse." We changed course.[2]

The individual with paranoid personality disorder needs to understand that the other person in their path may not be a battleship; he or she could be a lighthouse.

In this chapter, we seek to differentiate the sentinel type from paranoid personality disorder, as well as to offer guidance for the latter condition from both psychology and the Scriptures.

Characteristics of the Sentinel

Meet David, who has served for more than twenty years on the faculty of an eastern college. He is known for his independent thinking and irresistible logic. A quiet confidence coupled with a reserved demeanor, not to mention wry humor, have characterized his relationship with the hundreds of students taking his courses. He is not easily fooled by excuses masking his students' procrastination and undisciplined study habits. Nor does he hesitiate to question some of the decisions of the administration where he teaches. In faculty meetings, David listens carefully to arguments presented and, then, with sage replies challenges the assumptions of the presenters. If the meeting does not go his way, he has no qualms about leaving the room with a silent determination designed to display his protest. When any criticisms are lodged against David, he effectively dismisses them with a Stoic-like resolve. David is a highly esteemed professor, though he is capable of intimidating colleagues, administrators, and students alike. He is a valued ally unless, however, you cross him. Because he is dependable, he expects faithfulness in return.

David is a good example of the sentinel personality type. Oldham and Morris identify the following traits of such an individual, whom they label as "vigilant":

1. *Autonomy.* Vigilant-style individuals possess a resilient independence. They keep their own counsel, they require no outside reassurance or advice, they make decisions easily, and they can take care of themselves.
2. *Caution.* They are careful in their dealings with others, preferring to size up a person before entering into a relationship.
3. *Perceptiveness.* They are good listeners, with an ear for subtlety, tone, and multiple levels of communication.
4. *Self-defense.* Individuals with Vigilant style are feisty and do not hesitate to stand up for themselves, especially when they are under attack.
5. *Alertness to criticism.* They take criticism very seriously, without becoming intimidated.
6. *Fidelity.* They place a high premium on fidelity and loyalty. They work hard to earn it, and they never take it for granted.[3]

You can keep sentinels your allies by observing some important guidelines: (1) Respect them because, despite their tough exterior, in their hearts vigilants desire acceptance. (2) Accept their emotional aloofness by appreciating the logic that informs it, which might indeed work on your behalf if you prove to be a faithful friend. (3) Do not cower before them; rather be straightforward and transparent. In any event, you cannot fool them. (4) Do not try to intimidate or corner sentinels; they love a good argument. (5) Be patient and persevering in cultivating their friendship; it will pay off. (6) If you fail or offend the vigilant, be prepared to wait for their forgiveness. Knowing they tend to carry grudges will help you realistically deal with the relationship.

Paranoid Personality Disorder

The DSM-IV describes paranoid personality disorder as:

> A pervasive distrust and suspiciousness of others such that their motives are interpreted as malevolent, beginning by early adulthood and present in a variety of contexts, as indicated by four (or more) of the following:

1. suspects, without sufficient basis, that others are exploiting, harming, or deceiving him or her
2. is preoccupied with unjustified doubts about the loyalty or trustworthiness of friends or associates
3. is reluctant to confide in others because of unwarranted fear that the information will be used maliciously against him or her
4. reads hidden demeaning or threatening meanings into benign remarks or events
5. persistently bears grudges, i.e., is unforgiving of insults, injuries, or slights
6. perceives attacks on his or her character or reputation that are not apparent to others and is quick to react angrily or to counterattack
7. has recurrent suspicions, without justification, regarding the fidelity of spouse or sexual partner[4]

Ben: Profile of a Paranoid

Ben was a bivocational minister who was just as suited for a militia group. He pastored in a rural, midwestern town, far away from the hustle and bustle of the city. Ben thrived on questioning the government's every action, always suspicious that it secretly wanted to deprive Americans of their inalienable rights, especially the permission to own a gun. He constantly looked for innuendoes and nuances in the political arena that hinted at the coming takeover of the American people by the military. And anyone who disagreed with him, Ben labeled a communist! Such suspicion carried over into Ben's other job at the factory. There he firmly believed the boss was out to fire him (though that never happened). Not even Ben's mother or brother escaped his distrust. Often he spoke of their frustration with and rejection of him. Ben also doubted his wife's faithfulness to him, for no reason. Tragically Ben's suspicious nature ultimately drove his marriage to divorce. Moreover, Ben bore grudges against others, which precipitated his leaving both the pastorate and the factory. Worst of all, the accidental death of Ben's son created in him deep anger toward God.

Herod the Great

A much more serious illustration of paranoid personality disorder is found in Herod the Great (37–4 B.C.) of biblical fame. Four of the characteristics of such a condition pertained to Herod, based on the writings of Josephus, the Jewish historian (ca. A.D. 90). Admittedly, Herod the Great is an extreme case of paranoid personality disorder, but we nevertheless can learn from his example.

First, because Herod the Great was a half-Jew (or Idumean), his appointment as Rome's client king over Judea in 40 B.C. was sure to evoke criticism from Jews. To anticipate and compensate for any such reaction, Herod devoted his energies to establishing his reputation both in Israel and before Rome. Regarding the former, the client king engaged his country in massive and magnificent building projects, including Caesarea Maritime, the Herodium, Masada, and especially refurbishing the temple in Jerusalem. The last-mentioned project began in 19 B.C. (see John 2:20) and was not completed until A.D. 63, long after Herod's death (Josephus, *Antiquities* 20.19–20). In rebuilding the temple Herod intended to present himself as the new King Solomon (Josephus, *Antiquities* 15.380–7; 15.421–3). Moreover, Herod's attempt to commend himself to the Jews as their rightful king began early in his reign when he married Mariamne, a Hasmonean princess (the Hasmoneans had ruled Israel before the Roman takeover in 63 B.C.). Regarding his concern to impress the Roman overlords, Herod built Roman-style buildings, instituted gladiatorial sports, and set up images of Caesar in Jerusalem. Such actions could only stir up Jews to oppose him. The one ambition—pleasing the Romans—canceled out Herod's other attempt—pleasing the Jews. Josephus writes of this:

> For in the first place he established athletic contests ... in honor of Caesar and he built a theatre in Jerusalem, and after that a very large amphitheatre in the plain, both being spectacularly lavish but foreign to Jewish customs ... All round the theatre were inscriptions concerning Caesar and trophies of the nations which he had won in war, all of them made for Herod of pure

gold and silver.... Foreigners were astonished at the expense ... but to the natives it meant an open break with the customs held in honor by them. For it seemed glaring impiety to throw men to wild beasts for the pleasure of other men as spectators.... But more than all else it was the trophies that irked them (for they believed) that these were images surrounded by weapons ... against their national custom.[5]

Second, Herod was quick to react angrily to Jewish reactions against him. He stamped out any rumor of revolt, as his attempt to kill baby Jesus (a potential rival king) demonstrates (Matt. 2). On another occasion, having become aware of a foiled plot on his life, Herod "decided to hem the people in on all sides lest their disaffection should become open rebellion."[6] "Several measures for security he kept thinking up from time to time, and he placed garrisons throughout the entire nation so as to minimize the chance of [the Jews] taking things into their own hands."[7]

Third, Herod's suspicions and cruelty encompassed even his family, murdering his wife, Mariamne, three sons, mother-in-law, brother-in-law, uncle, and others. Preoccupation with safety from assassination motivated Herod to build the greatest monument to his paranoia—Masada, the wilderness fortress.

Fourth, Herod bore grudges so intensely against his enemies, real or perceived, all the way to his end. On his deathbed, for fear and rage that the Jews would not mourn his passing, the client king ordered the deaths of some Jews in order to ensure that the people would weep at his funeral.[8]

The example of Herod the Great is a morbid and extreme case of paranoid personality disorder. And, no doubt, Herod's cruel reputation was well-deserved. Nevertheless, the client king's predisposition to distrust others had the effect of creating self-fulfilling prophecies that only worsened the situation. Surely things would have been much different if Herod had experienced what people with paranoid personality disorder need the most, namely, peace with God, others, and themselves.

Possible Causes of Paranoid Personality Disorder

The professional literature on paranoid personality disorder gravitates to one of two theories concerning the cause of that condition. First, there is the "projection" theory.[9] Shapiro provides an explanation of this perspective:

The disorder is a result of "projection" of unacceptable feelings and impulses onto others. In theory, attributing unacceptable impulses to others rather than to oneself reduces or eliminates guilt over these impulses and thus serves as a defense against internal conflict. The psychoanalytical view, in essence, is that the individual inaccurately perceives in others that which is actually true of him or her, and, as a result, experiences less distress than would result from a more realistic view of self and others.[10]

On this reading, the individual's suspicions regarding others are rationalizations designed to reduce the person's subjective distress. Thus paranoid feelings are not central to the problem but rather a side effect of poor self-esteem.

The other view, the "cognitive" approach, disagrees, placing paranoia at the core of the condition.[11] Feelings of suspicion, distrust, and vigilance toward others are the result of a child's having been raised in an unhealthy, even unsafe environment. Parents who ridicule their children for any sign of weakness, lie to them, and even physically assault them create a hostile setting that encourages the development of paranoid personality disorder. In our opinion, the latter theory has the most to commend it.

Paranoid Personality Disorder and Other Personality Disorders

Paranoid personality disorder is one of the three types DSM-IV characterizes as the "odd cluster," along with schizoid and schizotypal personality disorders. All three share the following features: social isolation, pursuit of solitary activities, absence of intimate relationships, restricted expression of emotions.[12] We are thus justified in not treating schizoid and schizotypal personality disorders separately. Although the evidence is not conclusive, it does seem that extreme cases of paranoid personality disorder can lead to schizophrenia if left untreated.[13]

Millon has argued that paranoid personality disorder almost invariably covaries with other personality disorders. The "paranoid-narcissistic" subtype results from a strong belief in one's importance coupled with deficient social skills. When these individuals confront an environment that does not share their assumptions of superiority, the paranoid-narcissistic person retreats into fantasies of omnipotence, rather than acknowledging their weaknesses. The "paranoid-antisocial" condition results when a person projects hostile feelings on his or her environment, due to antagonism encountered in the nurturing process. The "paranoid-compulsive" disorder occurs because individuals were raised under rigid parental rules. Such perfect expectations render the child self-critical and withdrawn. Paranoia results when that individual attributes to others the hostility inherent in their harsh self-criticism.[14]

Paranoid over the Parousia

People with paranoid personality disorder, because of misgivings toward others, create anxiety, suspicion, and especially fear in those with whom they have contact. The last-mentioned reaction deserves special attention, for paranoid personality disorder, if undetected, can generate widespread panic. Even though paranoid personality disorder affects only approximately 5 percent of the population,[15] the influence of the condition can be enormous. Take, for example, modern-day doomsday prophets. We have argued elsewhere that such well-intentioned people are nevertheless prone to paranoia, especially regarding the Parousia (the Second Coming of Christ). Their books are selling into the millions, and their influence over people is astounding. Their message is captivating. With boldness and apparent precision, some of the more well-known contemporary religious prognosticators identify Russia (recent events having forced them to find a substitute for the Soviet Union, which no longer exists) with Gog and Magog (Ezek. 38–39), Red China with the "kings from the East" (Rev. 16:12–16) and the European Common Market with the "ten horns of the beast" (Rev. 13:1–10). Capitalizing on the Bible's relevance to modern society, these people commonly equate the locusts of Revelation 9:7–10 with Cobra helicopters and their deadly sting with nerve gas sprayed from the chopper's tail, or associate credit cards with the mark of the beast (666) of Revelation 13. Repeatedly these commentators of the modern era assert that we are living in the midst of the fulfillment of the signs of the times, as heralded by Jesus. Matthew 24:7 is seen to be fulfilled by famines like the ones in Ethiopia and Rwanda, earthquakes like those in California and Japan, and strife in the Middle East, Yugoslavia, and Los Angeles. Who can resist the appeal of the headlines in prophecy books showcased in many Christian bookstores: "Babylon Rebuilt"; "Ark of the Covenant Discovered"; "The Computer Beast in Belgium"; "Is Gorbachev Gog?" and "Is Carlos the Antichrist?"

Some of the prophets are downright funny—like the sincere doomsayer who observes that the false prophet who will make an image of the antichrist

(Rev. 13:14–15) will be better equipped to do so because of the development of robotics. Or the author who firmly believes that the white horse of Revelation 6:2 is a symbol of the United States, because its flag colors are red, white, and blue. Then there is the prophecy fanatic who sent a letter to a minister announcing that the building blocks of the end-time Jewish temple have all been cut and numbered and are presently being stored in K-Mart stores across the United States, awaiting the call to ship them to Jerusalem.[16]

However, the far-reaching ramifications of the power of doomsayers to bring about self-fulfilling prophecies is no laughing matter. The tragic end of self-proclaimed prophets like Jim Jones and David Koresh pales in significance compared to the global threat that could result from the wedding of contemporary prophetic crystal-ball readers and political theory. D. S. Russell, expert in Jewish-Christian apocalyptic literature, expresses it powerfully:

> One rather frightening by-product of this process of interpretation is that it is so easy to create the very situation which is being described so that the interpretation given brings about its own fulfillment. Russia, for example, is to be destroyed by nuclear attack—and scripture must be fulfilled! It needs little imagination to understand the consequences of such belief, especially if held with deep conviction by politicians and the military who have the power to press the button and to execute the judgment thus prophesied and foreordained.[17]

Treatment for Paranoid Personality Disorder

It is often noted that persons with paranoid personality disorder rarely enter into therapy, since they do not see their suspiciousness as a problem, are reluctant to accept help, and do not experience dysfunction such that they require involuntary treatment.[18] Nevertheless, individuals with this condition may seek help through therapy due to problems resulting from the disorder: difficulty in handling stress, conflicts with superiors or colleagues, marital struggles, or substance abuse. When an individual with paranoid personality disorder does seek treatment, for whatever reason, a skilled therapist will, with time, diagnose the true nature of the problem. After establishing a trust relationship with the client, the counselor's main goal will be to increase the counselee's sense of self-sufficiency:

The paranoid individual's intense vigilance and defensiveness are a product of the belief that constant vigilance and defensiveness are necessary to preserve his or her safety. If it is possible to increase the client's sense of self-efficacy regarding problem situations to the point that he or she is reasonably confident of being able to handle problems as they arise, then the intense vigilance and defensiveness seems less necessary and it may be possible for the client's symptomatology to substantially make it much easier to address his or her cognitions through conventional cognitive therapy techniques, and make it possible to persuade him or her to try alternative ways of handling interpersonal conflicts. Therefore, the primary strategy in the cognitive treatment of PPD is to work to increase the client's sense of self-efficacy before attempting to modify other aspects of the client's automatic thoughts, interpersonal behavior, and basic assumptions.[19]

From a spiritual perspective, the church can be of significant help to the individual afflicted with paranoid personality disorder. Two therapeutic steps can be taken toward such a person. First, the people of God should, as Ephesians 4:15 indicates, speak the truth in love to the overly vigilant. People with paranoid personality disorder need to hear the truth; they need to be exposed to the reality that they constantly engage in irrational thinking. One of the authors has done this regarding the alarmist prophecies of doomsayers, one manifestation of paranoid personality disorder. In our book, *Doomsday Delusions*, we call such foreboding predictions what they are—cognitive dissonance. Cognitive dissonance is a type of rationalization that occurs when people make predictions that are proven to be false. Instead of admitting being wrong, these folk recalculate their prophecies and intensify their efforts to bring them to pass. The history of the church is filled with such people, the most famous example of which was the Millerites. William Miller and his followers predicted that Christ would return on March 21, 1844. When the Parousia did not occur on that date, the Millerites reset the date for October 22, 1844. Unfortunately, a number of modern doomsday preachers are repeating the same phenomenon with regard to the year A.D. 2000, or shortly thereafter.[20]

On another occasion, one of the authors became friends with a young Christian who, as time progressed, began to share with others his many "strengths": military background, computer skills, swimming coach, spiritual warrior. After investigation, however, the young man's stories did not check out. In fact, he did not continue in the military, did not complete his computer training in college, and did not produce the champion swimmers he claimed. Concerning his calling to be a spiritual warrior, "Steve" planned on moving to Jerusalem to prepare for the Parousia. The author came to realize that Steve was paranoid—narcissistic—and straightforwardly told him so. Moreover, the young man was admonished to seek counseling.

But people with paranoid personality disorder need to hear the truth in love. They require unconditional acceptance, something they did not receive in childhood. Back to Steve. His parents were divorced when he was young; his mother, in particular was a harsh woman, who made a point of putting Steve in his place every moment she could. She berated him constantly, putting him on the defense. Little wonder that he grew up paranoid. In the church, even though we need to take what people with paranoid personality disorder say with a grain of salt, considering the source, we still must love them as God does—without question.

Second, we should assure the overly vigilant that God is sovereign and, therefore, can handle their worst fears. We need to encourage them to trust God and receive his peace (Gal. 5:22). The Spirit will cause tranquillity to prevail in the life of the one with paranoid personality disorder, if he or she lets him. Second Timothy 1:7 is just the word such individuals need, "For God has not given us a spirit of fear; but of power, and of love, and of a sound mind." Moreover, in being assured of God's control over the world and their existence, people with this condition need to take a step of faith by making charitable assumptions about others. They need to dare to believe that others, especially Christians, have their well-being in mind, with no ulterior motivation. Just as therapists can forge trusting relationships with those hurting from paranoid personality disorder, so with time can the people of God.

Conclusion

This chapter has been devoted to a discussion of paranoid personality disorder, its description, causes, and treatment. Truth, love, and peace can move people with this condition to the other side of the continuum, to being sentinels, whose lives are fulfilled and invaluable to the church. Perhaps a modern retelling of the old fable, Chicken Little, can help that process, in terms of both its humor and its insight. Chicken Little was picking up corn in the barnyard one day when an object fell from above and hit her on the head. It was a copy of a new bill to be passed in Congress that very day. It alarmed

Chicken Little that the document included a provision for barn-based health clinics. As Chicken Little ran by the red barn, her friends joined her, each with an interpretation of the dangers of the proposed bill. Henny Penny believed the bill endangered both the farm and religious speech. Cocky Locky interpreted the document to ban anything Christian. Groggy Froggy thought the bill went so far as to forbid worship in God. And on it went. Then the group encountered Foxy Woxy and told him of their plight. The fox invited them to go to his cave where they could send faxes to their representatives to protest the bill before it was voted on. They all agreed. As they followed Foxy Woxy, they ran into Wordy Birdy, who examined the document. She said, "This is simply a photocopy of the same bill that's been distributed for years; it's not real!"

"Then we got all worked up for nothing?" asked Chicken Little.

"I'm afraid so," said Wordy Birdy. "Your heavenly Father knows your frame and understands. Who of you by worrying can add a single hour to your life? As a matter of fact, you will surely be eaten if you continue on this path."

So Chicken Little, Henny Penny, Cocky Locky, and Groggy Froggy ran back to the barnyard.

As Wordy Birdy flew away, she noticed Foxy Woxy shaking his paw at her and lamenting her advice. For it was Foxy Woxy who had planted the bill in the barnyard and spread the rumor to strike fear into the animals and make them his noontime feast.[21]

◆ Seven ◆

The Maverick and Antisocial Personality Disorder

*B*oth personality types and disorders occur along a continuum. Sometimes the distinction between them is blurred in the eye of the beholder. The following response to the Apostle Paul's "job application" humorously demonstrates this point with regard to the maverick, the adventurous type, as related to the antisocial person:

> The Rev. Paul, Apostle
> Independent Missionary
> Corinth, Greece
> Dear Mr. Paul,
>
> We recently received an application from you for service under our mission board. We have made an exhaustive survey of your case and, frankly, we are surprised that you have been able to pass as a bonafide missionary. Note the following:
>
> 1. It is against our policy for a full-time missionary to do part-time secular work (we hear you are making tents on the side).

2. Further, is it true you have a jail record? Certain brethren report that you did two years' time at Caesarea and were also imprisoned in Rome.

3. Moreover, it is reported from Ephesus that you made so much trouble for the businessmen there that they refer to you as "the man who turned the world upside down." We feel such disregard for conformity has no place in missions today. We also deplore the "over the wall in a basket" episode at Damascus. We are appalled at your obvious lack of conciliatory behavior. Diplomatic men are not stoned or dragged out of city gates or assaulted by furious mobs. Have you ever considered that gentler words might gain you more friends? For your benefit we enclose a copy of Dalius Carnegus' book *How to Win Jews and Influence Greeks*. (We hear your friend Demas has a spare copy.)

4. Frankly, Mr. Paul, there has been some criticism of your preaching as well. Your sermons are repeatedly much too long for the churchgoing public. (We have conditioned them, you know, to stop listening after 30 minutes.) We hear that at one place you spoke until after midnight and a young man was so sleepy he even fell out of the window and broke his neck.

5. Finally, regrettably you do not meet our physical profile. Dr. Luke, the physician, reports that you are a thin little man, rather bald, frequently sick, and always so agitated regarding your churches that you sleep poorly. He indicates that you pace around the house praying half the night. Our ideal for all applicants is a healthy mind in a robust body. We believe that a good night's sleep will give you zest and zip so that you wake up full of zing.

We hesitate to inform you, Brother Paul, but in all our experience we have never met a candidate so opposite to the requirements of our mission board. If we should accept you, we would be breaking every principle of current missionary practice.

Most sincerely yours,
J. Flavius Fluffyhead
Secretary, Foreign Mission Board
(Adapted from Dave Carlstrom)

Now that's adventure for you! Before becoming a Christian, Paul was obsessive-compulsive, but his conversion transformed him into the apostle of the heart set free. Like Paul, the maverick is a daring soul. "Adrenaline Junky" is the label we apply to those endearing people whose spirit of risk and "throw caution to the wind" mentality set them apart from the rank and file of humanity. Where would we be without them? No ocean would have been crossed, no plane flown, no mountain climbed, no disease eliminated, and no enemy conquered. Writing of the maverick or adventurous individual, Oldham and Morris observe:

> The men and women with this personality style venture where most mortals fear to tread. They are not bound by the same terrors and worries that limit most of us. They live on the edge, challenging boundaries and restrictions, pitting themselves for better or for worse in a thrilling game against their own mortality. No risk, no reward, they say. Indeed, for people with the Adventurous personality style, the risk is the reward.[1]

But adventure can be too much of a good thing. Taken to extreme, daring and risk in the face of rules and at the expense of others can prove harmful, even deadly. Many of the inmates in our prisons provide ample testimony to the criminal behavior that can result when the maverick style gives way to antisocial personality disorder. Individuals with this condition, also known as psychopaths or sociopaths, are insensitive to the feelings of others and to the laws of society. Where others seek to build, they destroy. The major difficulty with this personality disorder is not identifying it but, rather, treating it. This chapter seeks to accomplish both, as we move on the continuum from the maverick personality to its negative counterpart, the antisocial personality disorder.

Oldham and Morris identify the following characteristics of the adventurous or maverick style:

1. *Nonconformity.* Men and women who have the Adventurous personality style live by their own internal code of values. They are not strongly influenced by other people or by the norms of society.
2. *Challenge.* To live is to dare. Adventurers love the thrill of risk and routinely engage in high-risk activities.
3. *Mutual independence.* They do not worry too much about others, for they expect each human being to be responsible for him or herself.

4. *Persuasiveness.* They are silver-tongued, gifted in the gentle art of winning friends and influencing people.
5. *Wanderlust.* They love to keep moving. They settle down only to have the urge to pick up and go, explore, move out, move on. They do not worry about finding work, and live well by their talents, skills, ingenuity, and wits.
6. *True grit.* They are courageous, physically bold, and tough. They will stand up to anyone who dares to take advantage of them.
7. *No regrets.* Adventurers live in the present. They do not feel guilty about the past or anxious about the future. Life is meant to be experienced *now.*[2]

Roger the "Reverent Renegade"

Roger exemplifies the adventurous, or maverick, personality. He was born a nonconformist. This was one of the traits that made him such an effective youth minister. As a student in his public high school, he bucked the crowd by following Christ. As a men's dormitory leader, he challenged the status quo system of his Christian college when he felt it needed revamping. Little wonder that many young people looked to Roger as a role model. Neither is it surprising that Roger never quite fit into a traditional church. If there had been a "bikers" congregation in his generation, Roger surely would have joined it or, most likely, led it!

For Roger, life was meant to be lived to its fullest. There was no place for the ordinary and the routine in his schedule. Roger's thirst for thrill propelled him along, from swimming in the ocean to building a cabin in the forests of Oregon. Football, racing, hiking, debating were but a few of the activities in his repertoire of excitement.

Roger was an independent thinker. The only person to whom he conformed was Christ! He truly did not care what others thought of him. Two symbols epitomize Roger's free spirit: his Corvette and the Fonz of *Happy Days.* Roger refused to be squeezed into the mold of the traditional Christian by driving a Ford or a Chevrolet. No, he dared to be different by buying a Corvette (which, by the way, he could not afford). When one of his supporters questioned whether he should own such an expensive car, Roger replied that youth ministers deserve the best! As far as Roger was concerned, he was a Corvette kind of a Christian. The other symbol of Roger's maverick spirit was the Fonz of *Happy Days*—that cool, teenage idol known for having his own mind and accent. Once at a school party, Roger dressed like the Fonz, marching to a different drummer, to the glee of his friends. Whether in ribald humor or reverent worship, Roger was his own person.

Another significant aspect to Roger's appeal was his persuasiveness. Articulate and animated, Roger could convince most to follow him, as he indeed hoped to follow Christ. Whether through an encouraging note or a raised voice, Roger commanded the respect of those to whom he was assigned in college and in ministry. Roger's love for travel also motivated others to be like him. But not everyone could keep up with his fast pace: from the streets of Chicago to the jungles of South America—one moment, mountain climbing; the next moment, scuba diving. People were amazed at how Roger could move from one place to another without prearranging for housing or finances.

Roger was bold; no one intimidated him. His six-foot-plus frame ensured that. Once, when he was in his Corvette, a not-so-fortunate automobile owner purposefully spun his car wheels in gravel ahead of Roger. This angered Roger, who caught up with the guy, cut him off at a turn, and proceeded to get out of his car to confront the fellow. An argument ensued, but cooler heads prevailed before there was a scuffle. On another occasion, a driver behind Roger leaned on his car horn at a stoplight because he did not think Roger moved quickly enough when the light turned green. Roger flung open his door and angrily stepped out of his car with the intent of engaging the driver. Roger's friend, however, deterred him from doing so, because it was late at night and they were in a dangerous part of town. At least that time Roger did not pursue the challenge.

Roger's motto was simple: the past is history, so forget it; the future is tomorrow, so don't worry about it; therefore "carpe diem!" This attitude was rooted in Roger's theology. If God took care of the past, then he will look out for the future. The Christian's task, then, is to serve Christ and others in the present!

Like Roger, the maverick personality has a number of strong points, including spontaneity, decisiveness in action, fearlessness, and enjoyment of life. But such individuals can get themselves, and others, into trouble if they do not temper their risks with calculation. Oldham and Morris offer the following suggestions to the adventuresome type:

1. Think from your head, not just your impulses.
2. Worry a little, to introduce some needed caution into your life.
3. Safeguard other people from the risks of your behavior.
4. Ask yourself: What do I want out of my life five to ten years from now?[3]

Antisocial Personality Disorder

At the other end of the spectrum of the maverick personality type is a group of people who take adventure too far. These folk get an adrenaline rush from breaking the law. Most of society operates by a moral code, or conscience, and believes that individuals should follow the rules of the land. This means people are expected to respect others and provide for their families. When people fail to live up to such standards, most feel guilty. Persons with antisocial personality disorder, however, neither feel obligated to obey the law nor do they experience remorse for wrongdoing to others. These folk love to beat the system. They want what they want, even if it belongs to others. Compassion is not a part of their vocabulary. DSM-IV describes such a condition as follows:

> There is a pervasive pattern of disregard for and violation of the rights of others occurring since age 15 years, as indicated by three (or more) of the following:
>
> 1. failure to conform to social norms with respect to lawful behaviors as indicated by repeatedly performing acts that are grounds for arrest
> 2. deceitfulness, as indicated by repeated lying, use of aliases, or conning others for personal profit or pleasure
> 3. impulsivity or failure to plan ahead
> 4. irritability and aggressiveness, as indicated by repeated physical fights or assaults
> 5. reckless disregard for safety of self or others
> 6. consistent irresponsibility, as indicated by repeated failure to sustain consistent work behavior or honor financial obligations
> 7. lack of remorse, as indicated by being indifferent to or rationalizing having hurt, mistreated, or stolen from another[4]

With this kind of profile, it is not surprising that many of the incarcerated criminals in our prisons have been diagnosed with antisocial personality disorder. In fact, antisocial personality disorder is second only to alcohol abuse as the driving force in the lives of convicted felons.[5]

But the majority of antisocial individuals have not been imprisoned; nevertheless, untreated, they pose a threat to society. Oldham and Morris' analysis of this condition is straightforward:

In public and private life, they use and abuse, outdo and out-
smart other people, and suffer little or no remorse. They can be
extremely shrewd and size up your weaknesses in no time. To
get what they want they will manipulate your conscience and
compassion. Somewhere along the Adventurous-Antisocial
continuum are people who commit professional ethics viola-
tions and think they're perfectly entitled, yet who lie convincingly when caught or confronted; those who take pride in saying
anything to a woman just to get her into bed, then blame her for
seducing them. They'll charm and disarm you, telling you what
you want to hear or what will touch your tender heartstrings.
An antisocial individual can con an elderly person out of his or
her meager savings and feel thrilled with the victory.[6]

Jake the Jailbird

One of the authors served as pastor of a church that Jake began attending. By his own admission, Jake had lived a rough and wild life. As a teenager,
he was busted for possession of drugs. Later he robbed a store and fired a gun
at a policeman (thankfully missing him, but not a streetlight). But Jake had an
excellent lawyer, so he was able to avoid conviction because of a technicality.
Jake later professed faith in Christ and started attending church. He seemed
to have become a model Christian by studying the Bible, witnessing, and giving.

Things, however, did not go well for long. Jake lost yet another job, this
one at a nearby factory. Moreover, he began having a premarital affair with a
woman (who attended Bible college)! Soon Jake moved out of town and
found another job. A few months later he contacted his former pastor about
the possibility of performing a wedding for Jake and his newfound girlfriend.
The pastor met with Jake and his fiancée. They seemed to be sincere and
desired to recommit their lives to Christ. The wedding date was set. When
that day came, the pastor arrived at the church (which had given him permission to officiate the wedding) only to find Jake drunk and his wife strung out
on drugs. Still, the pastor felt he had little recourse but to proceed with the
wedding.

That night was the last time the pastor saw Jake. Two years passed, and
the minister received a letter from him. It contained tragic news. Jake was
now divorced and, worse yet, was currently serving a life sentence in prison

for murdering a pimp over a prostitute. But there was a ray of hope in Jake's letter, for he expressed his grief for the crimes he had committed. In prison, he had resumed his walk with Christ through Bible study and fellowship with other Christian inmates.

What drives the antisocial? Six basic beliefs underly the behavior of such an individual:

1. Justification—"Wanting something or wanting to avoid something justifies my actions."
2. Thinking is believing—"My thoughts and feelings are completely accurate, simply because they occur to me."
3. Personal infallibility—"I always make good choices."
4. Feelings make facts—"I know I am right because I feel right about what I do."
5. The impotence of others—"The views of others are irrelevant to my decisions, unless they directly control my immediate consequences."
6. Low-impact consequences—"Undesirable consequences will not occur or will not matter to me."[7]

These self-serving beliefs govern the actions of antisocial people as well as dictate others' responses to them. Those with antisocial personality disorder typically generate three types of feelings in others. First, sometimes people experience anxiety in the presence of an antisocial individual. Such discomfort results because people feel manipulated and controlled by the mixed messages of individuals with antisocial personality disorder. Their flagrant violation of the rules contradictingly coupled with feigned interest in others keep the unwary off balance. When others do become aware of the true nature of the antisocial person, a second type of emotion often surfaces—anger. That anger can run the gamut from a defensive attitude to a shouting match, in the hopes of changing the lifestyle of the individual with antisocial personality disorder. "Because their behavior tends to be objectionable and even infuriating to others, ASPD patients may frequently get unsolicited counseling from others who want them to behave differently."[8] Third, other people ironically feel a sense of envy and even admiration at the bravado of antisocial people. Moreover, law-abiding folk sometimes wish they could get away with the breeches against society pyscho/sociopaths commit but for which they are not caught. Strangely, many of us find ourselves cheering at the movies for rogues, robbers, and renegades who elude the grasp of the law.

Causes of Antisocial Personality Disorder

What are the causes of antisocial personality disorder? Three factors contribute to the formation of such a condition: spiritual, environmental, and biological.

The perpetration of crime (detected or not) by such people is rooted in sin. Sin is breaking the law of God as it is expressed through the rules of society. Without adherence to these regulations (e.g., the Ten Commandments), there can be no civilization, only anarchy.

The first sin committed after the fall of Adam and Eve was antisocial in nature: Cain murdered Abel, his brother. Actually, Cain tragically serves as the first example (an extreme case to be sure) of antisocial personality disorder. Note how his actions fit the characteristics as DSM-IV delineates them:

1. Failure to conform to the law. The first remark about Cain in Genesis 4 concerns his failure to make an acceptable sacrifice before God. His crop offering as opposed to Abel's animal gift to God was subpar compared to the sacrificial system the whole of the Pentateuch prescribes. Moreover, Cain's offering was halfhearted, contrasted to that of his brother (vv. 1—5).

2. Irresponsible. Rather than confess his error, Cain became jealous of what his brother had—the praise of God (vv. 6—7). Yet Cain was not willing to pay the price for divine approval, namely, responsible behavior.

3. Aggressiveness and reckless disregard for others. Cain's jealousy gave way to uncontrolled anger, driving him to murder Abel (v. 8).

4—5. Deceitful. Cain demonstrated deceitfulness on two counts: First, he lured his brother Abel into the fields away from the view of others so he could murder him (v. 8). Second, when God asked Cain about his brother, he dismissed any knowledge of the incident, "Am I my brother's keeper?" (v. 9).

6. Failure to plan ahead. Cain's impetuous act of murder branded him for the rest of his life, confining him to be a wandering fugitive (vv. 10—16).

7. Lack of remorse. Like Judas of the New Testament, Cain showed no signs of genuine remorse and repentance. His agony was only that he was caught; his real concern was that his life would not be fulfilling (v. 13). The NIV well captures this point, "Confronted with his crime and its resulting curse, Cain responded not with remorse but with self-pity. His sin was uninterrupted: impiety (v. 3), anger (v. 5), jealousy, decep-

tion and murder (v. 8), falsehood (v. 9) and self-seeking (v. 13). The final result was alienation from God himself (vv. 14, 16)."[9]

Some believe that antisocial personality disorder is genetically caused. Seratonin (the body's chemical producing adrenaline) levels seem to be lower in antisocial people. Consequently, more risk or alarm is needed before they experience the "fight or flight" reaction than most people require.[10] Others argue that the cause of antisocial personality disorder is environmental: those individuals with this condition never bonded with a parent in their early childhood. Feelings of sensitivity and compassion toward others therefore do not easily occur in antisocial people.[11]

Treating Antisocial Personality Disorder

Diagnosing antisocial personality disorder is not difficult, but implementing a solution for the condition is. Three theories of treatment have been recommended: medical, rational, and spiritual. These options need not be mutually exclusive.

One proposed solution for this disorder has been to raise the level of seratonin in such people. This procedure has met with some success.[12]

Cognitive (rational) therapy attempts to move the counselee with antisocial personality disorder from the level of selfishness to the place where he or she realizes that it is in their best interest to consider the feelings and opinions of others. The chart on the following page illustrates how such a goal can be attained through dialogue with the counselor. The choice column, along with the respective advantages and disadvantages, moves toward more socially desirable behavior. In this case, the counselee's job situation was problematic.[13]

The objective of the therapist is eventually to lead the antisocial person to the highest level of behavior, namely, genuine consideration for the feelings and needs of others.

Charles Colson, former special counsel to President Richard Nixon, was imprisoned for his involvement in Watergate. While serving his term, Colson became a Christian. Upon his release, Colson began to champion the message that the only real cure for crime is spiritual conversion to Christ. Colson's organization, Prison Fellowship, has experienced great effectiveness in rehabilitating inmates throughout the U.S. That program involves three steps. First, the inmate must admit to his or her sin. In taking this stance,

Problem	Choice	Advantages	Disadvantages
Job. Demoted and placed on probation at work. Want to keep job.	Tell boss off and quit.	Easy. Get revenge.	Have to start job search again. Don't want to leave this one.
	Demand old job back.	Show I'm no wimp. (Might work.)	Risk getting fired now. Shows disrespect for boss.
	Find a way to make boss look bad for revenge.	Feel better about what they've done to me.	Boss might find out I made him look bad. His bad mood won't help me.
	Do as little as possible until they show more faith in me.	Low risk on my part. Get to take it easy for a while.	Boring. Probably won't get old job back very fast.
	Take a positive attitude and work my way back up the ladder.	Shows my interest in the company. Gives me something to do that is not so boring.	Company will get extra mileage out of me when they've already messed me up.

Colson dispels the "myth" (to use his term) that criminals commit crime primarily because of environmental factors. He writes:

> In their book the *Criminal Personality*, Stanton Samenow and Samuel Yochelson describe their study of 250 habitual criminals. When they began their study, Samenow and Yochelson held the conventional liberal view that criminals were victims of abuse and deprivation. They were looking for the social, psychological, or economic factor, or combinations of factors, that could be said to "cause" crime.
>
> To their surprise, they couldn't find any. They did find one thing that habitual lawbreakers have in common: Given a choice, they choose to break the law. And the answer—the only thing that can rehabilitate—is, Samenow and Yochelson wrote,

"the conversion" of the wrongdoer to a more responsible life. That is, a change of heart.

Norman Carlson, former director of the Federal Bureau of Prisons, also has said, "I've given up hope for rehabilitation because there is nothing we can do to force change on offenders. Change has got to come from the heart."[14]

Second, having acknowledged their sin, inmates are encouraged to trust in Christ. Having done that they are, third, placed in a discipleship group.[15] The results of the ministry of Prison Fellowship have been so phenomenal that parts of its program were incorporated into Florida's prison reform legislation passed in 1983.[16] Colson relates numerous testimonies of those inmates converted to Christ, along with the fruit of gentleness (though Colson does not call it such) that the Spirit wrought in their lives.[17]

At the end of the day, this is what the person with antisocial personality disorder needs—the gentleness of the Spirit that results from following Christ. This dynamic will help to activate the work of Christ in that person's (or any person's) experience: "the LORD has anointed me/ to preach good news to the poor. /He has sent me to . . . proclaim freedom for the captives/ and release for the prisoners" (Isa. 61:1).

Conclusion

After a long, troubled past, this is what Jake, whom we referred to earlier in this chapter, experienced, even if in the midst of serving a life sentence. We believe that medical treatment and cognitive therapy are helpful approaches to those with antisocial personality disorder. Ultimately, however, it is only through the power of the Spirit of Christ, that insensitive, even law-breaking, people can be transformed into gentle men and women. In the case of the antisocial individual, conversion to Christ and the enabling strength of the Spirit can help them to become the maverick type of persons they were created to be, folk who thrive on adventure and even take calculated risks in order to help others realize their potential in Christ—like our friend Roger.

◆ Eight ◆

The Rebel and Borderline
Personality Disorder

The rebel personality or, as Oldham and Morris label it—the "mercurial style," is filled with vivaciousness and life. When you are with these folk, fasten your seat belt and hold on to your hat! You never know what to expect from them, because their highs and lows take you on a roller-coaster ride of emotions. Seven traits characterize the rebel:

1. *Romantic attachment.* Mercurial individuals must always be deeply involved in a romantic relationship with one person.
2. *Intensity.* They experience a passionate, focused attachment in all their relationships. Nothing that goes on between them and other people is trivial, nothing is taken lightly.
3. *Heart.* They show what they feel. They are emotionally active and reactive. Rebel types put their hearts into everything.
4. *Unconstraint.* They are uninhibited, spontaneous, fun-loving, and undaunted by risk.

5. *Activity.* Energy marks a Mercurial style. These individuals are lively, creative, busy, and engaging. They show initiative and can stir others to activity.

6. *Open mind.* They are imaginative and curious, willing to experience and experiment with other cultures, roles, and value systems and to follow new paths.

7. *Alternate states.* People with Mercurial style are skilled at distancing or distracting themselves from reality when it is painful or harsh.[1]

Cindy, the Rebel

Meet Cindy, the rebel. Here is a person who is a committed Christian and who, to put it figuratively, "grabs all the gusto" she can out of life. Just ask her loving husband who, for more than twenty years of marriage, is still trying to catch his breath from keeping up with her!

Their relationship began years ago in the South when Cindy became an employee at Larry's antique shop. Cindy fell madly in love with Larry and, after a whirlwind romance, they were married. Immediately, Larry pulled up stakes, sold his business, moved to California, and opened another shop there.

While many brides might have had difficulty leaving family and friends so soon after their wedding, not so with Cindy. The challenges of a different setting appealed to her. Nor was she daunted by their just as quick return to the South when things did not work out on the West Coast.

After a few years of marriage, Larry became a Christian and, together with Cindy and their two sons, entered into full-time youth ministry. Their financial support was based almost solely on the giving of others.

None of the obstacles of meager living, however, detracted from Cindy's zest for life. Her enthusiastic attitude would prove vital in the future, as her husband made a number of moves in the ministry—from youth minister to associate pastor to senior pastor. In fact, Cindy's energetic and all-heart mind-set greatly complemented her husband's service to the churches.

Cindy's passionate commitment to key relationships in the ministry endeared herself to the people of God. On one occasion, she fasted for a number of days on behalf of an ailing friend. Moreover, her zealous activity kept all associated with her extremely busy as she started one program after another.

Cindy's imagination and creativity ensured that there would always be new visions of service for Christ, fueled by her non-status quo approach toward life. Never mind that she could rather easily "lose it" in a conversation and tell a person exactly what she felt. Such instability and fluctuation between intense commitment and intimidating show of anger and tears toward the same individual always kept others guessing what to expect from Cindy. Nevertheless, her uninhibited, spontaneous, fun-loving spirit easily won a person back (until the next outburst)!

On one occasion, when Cindy confided in her pastor that much of her life was driven by extremes—ups and downs—without being able to find a happy medium, the minister suggested that she explore the possibility that she might be unknowingly suffering from past hurts. Not long thereafter, Cindy and Larry were called to another church position some distance away, making difficult further discussion of the matter with her pastor. But the move seemed to be good for Cindy, providing her with new opportunities, challenges, and more occasions to display her affectionate rebel style.

Oldham and Morris offer some helpful advice for those in a relationship with the rebel, or mercurial, personality:

1. Step up on your pedestal. The Mercurial person wants and needs to idealize and overvalue you. Enjoy his or her admiration of the best, noblest, and most romantic aspects of your character, and let your relationship with this person bring out the best in you.

2. Step down from your pedestal. You may need to remind the Mercurial person—and yourself—rather regularly that although you appreciate his or her feelings and expectations, you are after all a mere mortal who is at times selfish, uninteresting, weak, and even unkind. Ask for acceptance and understanding of all aspects of you.

3. Don't be surprised or thrown by the Mercurial person's changeable moods, and try not to overreact to them.

4. Mercurial individuals often expect you to understand what they are reacting to and are hurt when you don't figure it out. Save time and trouble: ask for an explanation.

5. Mercurial individuals can be impulsive and excessive and may let the necessary business of life slide. You be the responsible one if you're good at that.

6. Show your warmth, love, devotion, and dedication frequently. Hearing how much you love them and how special they are to you is important to Mercurial people. The Mercurial person in your life may be quite a handful, for these people are tempestuous, and what they want from you can be very hard to provide. But they can be courageous, interest-

ing, exciting, and can show you a deep and profound love unlike any you have experienced before. Openly appreciate them for all that.[2]

Rebel types can benefit from two suggestions:

1. Objectify your emotions. Because mercurial people have the tendency to be driven by their emotions, it would help them to take moments during the day to distance themselves from their feelings. In doing so, rebels can examine their emotions objectively, thus depriving them of control over their lives. The goal in this is, of course, not to deny one's feelings but rather to take charge of those feelings in a rational way. This exercise will at first seem unnatural to the rebel type, but with practice it begins to feel more comfortable; and the strategy works.

2. Do not polarize people. A key characteristic along the continuum of the rebel type (a healthy type) to borderline personality disorder (an unhealthy condition) is dichotomous thinking. The latter mentality categorizes everything as right or wrong, black or white. There is no room for moderation in such thinking. Hence people with borderline personality disorder perceive themselves and others in stark contrast: now acceptable, now unacceptable. To remedy this, the individual with this condition needs to work at neither idealizing nor vilifying others and themselves.

A decrease in dichotomous thinking often results in a notable decrease in the frequency of sudden mood swings and a decrease in the intensity of clients' emotional reactions, due to their evaluating problem situations in less extreme terms. However, the clients can attain additional control over emotional responses through increasing their ability to look critically at their thoughts in problem situations, and by learning adaptive ways to express emotions.[3]

Borderline Personality Disorder

When the dichotomous thinking of the rebel goes unchecked, it could develop into borderline personality disorder, a frustrating and lonely way of functioning in the world. The DSM-IV describes borderline personality disorder as:

A pervasive pattern of instability of interpersonal relationships, self-image, and affects, and marked impulsivity beginning by early adulthood and present in a variety of contexts, as indicated by five (or more) of the following:

1. frantic efforts to avoid real or imagined abandonment
2. a pattern of unstable and intense interpersonal relationships characterized by alternating between extremes of overidealization and devaluation
3. identity disturbance: markedly and persistently unstable self-image or sense of self
4. impulsivity in at least two areas that are potentially self damaging (e.g., spending, sex, substance abuse, reckless driving, binge eating)
5. recurrent suicidal behavior, gestures, or threats, or self-mutilating behavior
6. affective instability due to a marked reactivity of mood (e.g., intense episodic dysphoria, irritability, or anxiety usually lasting a few hours and only rarely more than a few days)
7. chronic feelings of emptiness or boredom
8. inappropriate, intense anger or difficulty controlling anger (e.g., frequent displays of temper, constant anger, recurrent physical fights)
9. transient, stress-related ideation or severe dissociative symptoms[4]

Bob the Borderline

The telltale sign of borderline personality disorder is confusion and an out-of-control life: mentally, emotionally, vocationally, interpersonally, and spiritually. Such was Bob's situation. Bob came from a dysfunctional family. His father was a heavy drinker and prone to gambling and violence. Bob's father raised his seven children inconsistently. To some of them he was an adoring fan; to others, like Bob, he was a fierce disciplinarian. Bob could hardly wait to leave home, even if it meant joining the Navy.

As a man in his twenties, Bob seemed to find stability and security in the military; he planned to make it a career. But a series of relationships with women, one of which culminated in a divorce, caused Bob to change his plans. Thereafter, he never seemed to be able to find the "right" job. A couple of years later Bob fell in love with Debbie and, after a quick romance, married her. No sooner were they married than Bob moved out of state to take a welding position. But after a year he was laid off.

Bob tried numerous employment opportunities. None of them lasted long. His drinking, interpersonal conflicts (sometimes of a physical nature) with coworkers and employees, along with poor self-esteem, made any job impermanent. Strangely, however, even though Bob suffered from a low opinion of himself, he often felt superior to others. Yet his grandiose dreams never seemed to materialize.

When Bob was not drinking, it would have been difficult to find a more humble, even dependent man. At times, he felt overwhelmed by loneliness and a sense of abandonment. Bob's self-esteem was not helped by his weight problem (he was only 5'9" and weighed 270 pounds), caused by prolonged eating binges. The undisciplined eating habits, along with his alcoholism, was responsible for the onset of diabetes. Bob tried everything in order to put his life together: Alcoholics Anonymous, medical treatment, and even church. But when Bob's Christian friends told him how much God loved him, he simply could not believe it. Bob's second marriage ended in divorce, and he died shortly thereafter, at the rather young age of fifty-four. After years of consuming alcohol, cirrhosis of the liver claimed his life. He passed away having accumulated no wealth or material goods to pass on to his heirs. Bob's former wife and children loved him to the end, but they had no idea how to make his life better.

The borderline individual, like other personality disorders discussed in this work, has difficulty coping with life. Young identifies the basic beliefs that form the borderline person's maladaptive way of perceiving reality, schemes developed in childhood[5] (See chart on page 109).

Borderline personality disorder is defined as an enduring pattern of perceiving, relating to, and thinking about the environment and oneself in which there are problems in a variety of areas including interpersonal behavior, mood, and self-image.[6] The most striking features of such a condition are the intensity of emotional reactions and the changeability of symptoms present in the borderline individual. To the novice counselor, borderline personality disorder is difficult to diagnose because of the variability of the condition, but to experienced therapists such diversity is precisely the crucial indicator that their clients are borderline. Clinicians look for the following symptoms in three key areas:

In Presenting Problems and Symptoms:

1. A diverse assortment of problems and symptoms, which may shift from week to week

Early Maladaptive Schema	Possible Expression
Abandonment/Loss	"I'll be alone forever. No one will be there for me."
Unlovability	"No one would love me or want to be close to me if they really got to know me."
Dependence	"I can't cope on my own. I need someone to rely on."
Subjugation/lack of individuation	"I must subjugate my wants to the desires of others or they'll abandon me or attack me."
Mistrust	"People will hurt me, attack me, take advantage of me. I must protect myself."
Inadequate self-discipline	"It isn't possible for me to control myself or discipline myself."
Fear of losing emotional control	"I must control my emotions or something terrible will happen."

2. Unusual symptoms or unusual combinations of symptoms
3. Intense emotional reactions that are out of proportion to the situation
4. Self-punitive or self-destructive behavior
5. Impulsive, poorly planned behavior that is later recognized as foolish, "crazy," or counterproductive
6. Confusion regarding goals, priorities, feelings, sexual orientation, etc.

In Interpersonal Relationships:

1. Lack of stable intimate relationships (possibly masked by stable nonintimate relationships or relationships that are stable as long as full intimacy is not possible)
2. A tendency to confuse intimacy and sexuality

In Therapy:

1. Frequent crises, frequent telephone calls to the therapist, or demands for special treatment in scheduling sessions, making final arrangements, etc.
2. Extreme or frequent misinterpretations of therapist's statements, intentions, or feelings

3. Unusually strong reactions to changes in appointment time, room changes, vacations, or termination of therapy
4. Low tolerance for direct eye contact, physical contact, or close proximity
5. Unusually strong ambivalence on many issues
6. Fear of change or unusually strong resistance to change[7]

Samson: A Man Out of Control

Only one thing is worse than a man out of control, and that is the strongest man being out of control—Samson! At least five of the characteristics of borderline personality disorder jump out from the chapters of Scripture devoted to describing his life, Judges 13—16.

1. Samson's life from beginning to end was marked by unstable interrelationships, especially concerning his romantic escapades. He saw a Philistine woman (the Philistines were the archenemies of the Israelites), and he ordered his parents to bring her to him (14:1—8). When that relationship came to a tragic end (the woman was killed by the Philistines in retaliation for Samson's revenge on them for figuring out his riddle (14:9—15:6), Samson impetuously took up with a prostitute (16:1—2). That relationship failing, the Herculean judge entered an ill-advised romance with Delilah, and the rest of the story is history (16:1—30).
2. Samson was impulsive. This is nowhere more evident than in his reckless abandonment of his Nazirite vows. Samson, chosen to be separate and holy unto God, was not to eat or touch anything unclean or to shave his hair (cf. Num. 6:1—21 with Judg. 13:1—24). Tragically, on the spur of the moment, Samson ate honey from a dead (therefore unclean) lion (one he had earlier killed, 14:8—9). The same restlessness drove the young judge to cohabitate with a harlot, an unclean person (16:1). And, ultimately, Samson's disregard for his Nazirite vow inexorably led him to imprisonment and blindness because he divulged to Delilah the secret of his strength, namely, his long hair (ch. 16).
3. Interspersed with Samson's impulsiveness was his inappropriate, even violent, display of anger. He thoughtlessly taunted a riddle before thirty townspeople during his wedding week. When they coaxed the answer from Samson's bride, the reckless judge killed thirty Philistines and, to fulfill his promise to those who discovered the key to the riddle, gave their clothing to the townspeople (ch. 14). Samson's propensity to violence erupted again after his father-in-law gave his wife away to

the Philistines. In rage, Samson set three hundred pairs of foxes afire in the Philistine fields, then murdered his wife and father-in-law. Consequently, Samson slew hundreds of those Philistines (15:9–20). Next, Samson got in a fight with the men at Gaza who tried to trap him at the harlot's house (16:1–3). Headstrong and out of control, Samson found himself embroiled in conflict after conflict.

4. Samson was driven by a sense of boredom, behind which was emptiness. He moved in and out of relationships, picked fights, and maintained an inconsistent walk with God. Samson needed to learn the truth stated years later by Augustine, "Our hearts are restless until they find their rest in Thee."

5. Finally, Samson's propensity to self-destruction came to a head when, imprisoned and blinded by the Philistines in the aftermath of Delilah's deception, the unstable judge, now with his hair regrown long, pulled down the pillars of the pagan temple, killing himself and all therein.

Causes of the Borderline Condition

Of all the personality disorders, the borderline condition is today capturing the most research and clinical interest among mental health professionals. Some 20 percent of patients in psychiatric wards suffer from this disorder. Secondary causes often motivate borderline people to submit to professional help, such as suicidal tendencies, substance abuse, and depression.[8]

What is the cause of borderline personality disorder? While some researchers point to a genetic disposition behind the mood swing that produces the borderline's maelstrom of symptoms,[9] more certain is the influence of a dysfunctional homelife. Oldham and Morris identify the role of such a background:

Many Borderline women and men come from disturbed or broken families in which there were alcoholism, abuse, violence, and traumatic separations. As children, many experienced extreme physical or verbal brutality. Studies have found the rate of childhood sexual abuse to be as high as 70 percent of borderline individuals. Other research has determined that 25 percent of individuals with Borderline personality disorder are also diagnosed with post-traumatic stress disorder, which suggests that there is a common role of trauma in both disorders.

The vast majority of all Borderline individuals reveal a history of adverse, inconsistent, and unpredictable parenting. Some come from families that appeared well-functioning on the surface, but in which one or both parents hampered or punished the child's earliest attempts at establishing an independent identity and simultaneously discouraged closeness and intimacy.[10]

Borderline people generate in others feelings of confusion and intimidation. The former emotion results because borderline individuals so quickly and unpredictably switch from positive attitudes like love and commitment to negative expressions of anger and hostility. Consequently, intimidation arises within those in the presence of the borderline person.

Treatment of the Borderline

Help is available for those with borderline personality disorder. Crisis management is the goal for short-term inpatient or outpatient programs and therapies, while psychotherapy over a period of about four years can effect significant changes within the borderline individual.[11] The main objective of long-term counseling is to correct the dichotomous thinking that so adversely dominates the person with borderline personality disorder. Moreover, the breakthrough trauma-treatment EMDR (Eye Movement Desensitization Reprocessing) may well prove to accelerate borderline therapy. Not to be omitted from the discussion of solutions for this disorder is the fruit of self-control, which the Spirit can give to borderline people. By his power, these people can learn to "be still and know God." With the aid of Christ, along with other helps mentioned, borderline individuals can overcome impulsivity and confusion. As a result, they can experience objectivity in thinking and consistency in attitude and action.

Conclusion

We conclude this chapter by calling attention to King Solomon of old, whose book—Ecclesiastes—provides a profile of a borderline individual who, after years and years of turmoil, found tranquillity. "From vanity to virtue" might well characterize the king's spiritual journey. Note Solomon's "privileged" existence:

1. Because the same destiny seemed to overtake both righteous and evil, the king felt abandoned to an unjust fate (9:3–10).

2. His unstable and multitudinous relationships with women are common knowledge—a harem of a thousand wives and concubines, who turned his heart from God (1 Kings 11:1—6).

3. Solomon's impulsivity with wine (2:3), women (2:8), and spending (2:4—9; 5:8—17) are also well-known.

4. The king often encountered despair because of the vanity and futility of life, prompting within him sustained longing for death (4:2; 6:3).

5. Solomon's mood swings, which alternated between admiration for wisdom and a sense of helplessness before folly, dominate the Book of Ecclesiastes, creating confusion and fear within the reader.

6. The keynote statement of the Book of Ecclesiastes in 1:1—11 bespeaks an author driven by emptiness and boredom, whose life is described as chasing after the wind.

But just when the reader is ready to give up hope, Solomon arrives at the true reason for living:

"Now all has been heard;
    here is the conclusion of the matter:
Fear God and keep his commandments,
    for this is the whole duty of man.
For God will bring every deed into judgment,
    including every hidden thing,
    whether it is good or evil."
(Ecclesiastes 12:13—14)

Here in this Scripture we have the first spiritual behavior modification program. According to verse 13, humans are to do what is right before God. Obeying God is humankind's duty. People with borderline personality disorder especially need to hear this message for, in the final analysis, objective thinking and consequently righteous living (self-control) are what these people desperately need. To help motivate such behavior, verse 14 promises a reward from the Creator for those who dedicate themselves to virtuous living. Stated another way, God can help such people be rebels with a cause instead of borderline and out of control.

◆ Nine ◆

The Healthy Personality

We have focused on personality disorders, recognizing the difficulties they pose in relating in a healthy way to others and the impact that such interpersonal problems have on our lives. Personality disorders distort people's perceptions of God, themselves, and others, eclipsing their God-given strengths. We have briefly examined the particular fruit of the Spirit that can restore these individuals to a healthy way of functioning in the world, enabling them to participate fully in life in a joyful way in which they can meet both their own needs and reach out to others.

Of course, this is not usually an immediate or overnight "cure." While not underestimating the power of God to work in instantaneous, permanent, life-changing ways in a person's life (which we have seen occur primarily when an intense, traumatic experience takes place, completely changing an individual's world), change more often takes place gradually, through an openness to God's truth, which permeates people's lives and gives them a new view of themselves and others. They are thereby liberated to live a life of authenticity.

Personality disorders are not simply a spiritual problem that can be eliminated, for example, by admonishing someone to have more faith or to try to be more obedient to God. That would be a gross oversimplification of what is involved in a personality disorder, and deep suffering results from well-meaning, but misinformed pastors and others who take this approach. We have frequently seen the existence of personality disorders that have resulted from the experience of abuse, and simply "trying harder" on the person's part does not remove the destructive effects of the condition.

Long-term, intensive counseling with a professional is often needed to work through the experiences and issues that have resulted in a personality disorder, and reprogramming of the mind with truth and acting on that truth is often a daily (if not hourly) struggle for some time. However, we can attest to the fact that the struggle is worth the effort and that the love and power of God are indeed there to sustain the individual. Gradually, the individual experiences freedom from negative, destructive characteristics that once ruled his or her life and experiences a deeper joy and satisfaction in life than he or she ever thought possible.

In this conclusion, we will examine the characteristics of the healthy personality to which we all strive and see how Jesus personified these traits. He is indeed a magnificent role model. In addition, we will further discuss the fruit of the Spirit and how these attributes enable us to become emotionally healthy individuals.

Much has been written regarding the traits which reflect a healthy personality, for example, that of loving and accepting oneself and caring deeply for others. Respect for oneself and other people is evidenced by compassionate, yet nevertheless, limit-setting behavior in which emotional, physical, and spiritual needs can be met. Taking charge of one's own behavior, and allowing others to take responsibility for their behavior, is evident. A genuineness is present in the individual's life; pretense is abandoned, and phoniness in others is detected and rejected as well. Those with a healthy personality have a strong sense of purpose in life. They believe that they are meant to fulfill a certain "mission" to make life better in some way, whether great or small—a special task which gives their lives joy and meaning. While not necessarily on such a grand scale as Mother Theresa or Martin Luther King, Jr., they believe that they are meant to contribute in their own way, that they have been created to accomplish something significant with their lives. These dreams uplift and empower themselves and others. They view every person with whom they come into contact as unique and important; and a belief in the equality of all individuals is evidenced by their behavior.

They are also liberated, unafraid to express nontraditional views or to conduct themselves in unorthodox ways (as long as they are Christian), and thus can frequently go against societal expectations. They display an open-ness in considering other viewpoints but are less dependent on others' approval and thus form convictions based on what they ultimately believe to be the truth.

Not consumed by events of the past or obsessed with the future, they are fully present in the here and now, savoring life and finding joy and meaning in simple, everyday pleasures. While they are not necessarily humorous in a tra-ditional sense, they often possess a great sense of humor in their appreciation of life.

In all of this, Jesus is our consummate role model, exemplifying these very traits of the healthy personality. Let's look at four aspects of the healthy personality which Jesus personifies:

1. *Loving others.* One aspect of a healthy personality is showing respect and appreciation for others and forming deep, personal relationships. Jesus' life illustrates these traits. For example, in John 11, we read the account of the death of Lazarus and the grief which Jesus experienced due to the loss of his friend and of the rejoicing that occurred as Jesus raised Lazarus from the dead. John 13 speaks of Jesus' sacrificial love for his disciples as he washed their feet, his sadness over knowing he had but a little time yet to spend with these friends, and his exhortation to them to love one another as he loved them. The ultimate gift of love he gave was that of his life in order to purchase freedom for all of humanity.

2. *Purpose in life.* Individuals with a healthy personality have a goal, a "mission," or a philosophy of life around which their entire being revolves. They feel their life has a unique purpose and their behavior is consistent with reaching this objective. In recent years, people such as Steven Covey have popularized and adapted this concept, as they encourage people to formulate mission statements for themselves per-sonally, as families, and as organizations, in order to examine the unique ways in which their talents can be used to make meaningful contribu-tions to the world.[1]

Jesus' life was one of purpose and meaning. He exemplified love in action. For example, in Matthew 4:18–22, Jesus called the first disciples; and Matthew 4:23 speaks of Jesus' mission, as he taught and preached in the syn-agogues and healed the sick. As his fame grew, many people were brought to him to heal. His influence and purpose in life, however, extended far beyond the geographical area in which he traveled and the time he spent on earth. Matthew 5:17 tells of that ultimate mission: fulfilling the law and paying the penalty for sin by sacrificing his own life.

3. *Independent thinking.* Individuals with a healthy personality are seekers of truth. They are open-minded in considering others' opinions and perspectives but make decisions based on their own values. These convicitions are not based on what is popular in their society or culture, and thus their beliefs and behavior may, at times, be unconventional. When important social issues are involved, persons with a healthy personality choose integrity rather than popularity. Popular public opinion does not rule their lives, and they are willing to pay the price for acting in ways that are consistent with their beliefs, even when such action may alienate them from others.

Jesus was an independent thinker. His unconventional views frequently exasperated and infuriated the religious leaders, while the common people were drawn to his message of love and forgiveness. One of the most familiar examples of Jesus' actions, which showed his willingness to go against expectations of his day, took place in the temple. Matthew 21 records how the flagrant misuse of the temple provoked Jesus' anger. He overturned the tables and benches used for selling the wares. He had also provoked religious establishment's wrath on numerous other occasions, for example, when he and his disciples picked some grain on the Sabbath and also healed on the Sabbath (Matt. 12; Luke 13), which constituted breaking the Hebrew laws.

Jesus' treatment of all people as equals before God went against the popular mores of his day. He elevated the status of women and children, showing them love and compassion, and treating them as equals. Jesus' gathering little children around him and his speaking to the woman at the well, a social outcast, evidence his highly unconventional behavior when important social issues were at stake. Jesus first appeared after his resurrection to a woman, and we know that a number of women were followers of Jesus, having traveled with him and his disciples.

4. *Authentic living.* An integral characteristic of those with a healthy personality is authenticity—honesty and lack of pretense in dealing with others. Their actions reflect their integrity. Being in the presence of genuine individuals with whom you know exactly where you stand is always refreshing. They detect phoniness in others and are able to confront people with the truth in a spirit of love. They are less dependent

on others' approval for a sense of worthiness and belonging, deriving their self-esteem from the knowledge that as a child of God they have nonnegotiable self-worth. They are seekers of the truth, and their actions match their convictions.

Jesus' actions are anything but that of a "pretender." In Matthew 23, Jesus railed against the religious leaders of his day, exposing their hypocrisy. It would have been far easier (and safer) for Jesus to have not directly antagonized these individuals by revealing their lives of deceit and persecution of the righteous. Numerous other occasions such as these are recorded, for example, in Mark 12:38–40 in which Jesus spoke of the way the teachers of the law viewed themselves as superior to others and thus demanded the places of honor in a conspicuous show of pretense, and in Luke 12 where Jesus criticized the Pharisees and predicted their future demise as they would be called to accountability by God, before whom all is revealed.

Jesus, the epitome of a healthy personality, was also one filled with the fruit of the Spirit. Such qualities can be seen to meet the respective needs of the various personality disorders discussed in this study. The peace that Jesus promised to his disciples in the upper room, in the face of adversity and hostility, is what the paranoid individual desperately needs. Jesus' gentleness in dealing with others is what is missing in the antisocial person. The borderline individual can better get a grip on life by imbibing Jesus' self-control, powerfully demonstrated in his obedient life to God. The histrionic can embrace personal responsibility and commitment to people other than themselves by learning from Jesus' faithfulness, manifested so beautifully in his death for humanity. Jesus' goodness and mercy to sinners and the oppressed can set narcissists free from their selfishness. The joy of Christ can calm the troubled, intimidated soul of the avoidant, while Jesus' meekness, coupled with power, can make the dependent one independent by relying on God. And the grace of Christ, evident in the cross, is surely what the obsessive-compulsive needs to reaffirm daily.

Of course, all of us need all of the fruit of the Spirit of Christ, but those with personality disorders can especially benefit from those qualities that pertain to their respective weaknesses. And, finally, the starting place in all of this is love—love for God through Christ—from which the other fruits of the Spirit blossom.

Endnotes

Introduction

1. John M. Oldham and Lois B. Morris, *The New Personality Self-Portrait* (New York: Bantam Books, 1995), 16.
2. Ibid., 16–24.
3. George Howe Colt and Anne Hollister, "Were You Born That Way?" *Life Magazine,* April 1998, 40.
4. James Dobson, *Parenting Isn't for Cowards* (Waco, Tex.: Word, 1987), 24.
5. Ken Voges and Ron Braund, *Understanding How Others Misunderstand You: A Unique and Proven Plan for Strengthening Personal Relationships* (Chicago: Moody Press, 1995), 28.
6. Ibid., 28–29.
7. Oldham and Morris, 22–24.
8. Ibid., 4–5, 21.
9. Reprinted with permission from the *Diagnostic and Statistical Manual of Mental Disorders,* Third Edition. Copyright 1980 American Psychiatric Association, 305.
10. Eugene Kennedy and Sara C. Charles, M.D., *On Becoming a Counselor: A Basic Guide for Nonprofessional Counselors.* New Expanded Edition (New York: Crossroad Publishing Company, 1995), 220. Reprinted with permission from the *Diagnostic and Statistical Manual of Mental Disorders,* Third Edition. Copyright 1980 American Psychiatric Association.
11. Ibid., 221.
12. Ibid., 220–21.
13. Ibid., 221.

14. Theodore Millon, *Disorders of Personality, DSM III, Axis II* (New York: John Wiley and Sons, 1981), 75.

15. Oldham and Morris, 391.

16. Wayne Edward Oates, *Behind the Masks: Personality Disorders in Religious Behavior* (Philadelphia, Penn.: Westminster Press, 1987), 124.

17. Ibid., 108.

18. Ibid.

19. Ibid.

20. Ibid., 127.

21. Ibid., 132–33.

22. Ibid., 135.

23. Millon, 90.

24. Kennedy and Charles, 222.

Chapter 1

1. John M. Oldham and Lois B. Morris, *The New Personality Self-Portrait* (New York: Bantam Books, 1995), 77.

2. Robert Hemfelt, Paul Meier, and Frank Minirth, *We Are Driven* (Nashville, Tenn.: Thomas Nelson, 1991), 8.

3. Ibid., 6.

4. Ibid., 7–8.

5. Oldham and Morris, 77.

6. Ibid., 65.

7. Aaron T. Beck, Arthur Freeman, and Associates, *Cognitive Therapy of Personality Disorders* (New York: Guilford Press, 1990), 42, 46.

8. Ibid., 54.

9. Eugene Kennedy and Sara C. Charles, M.D., *On Becoming a Counselor: A Basic Guide for Nonprofessional Counselors,* New Expanded Edition (New York: Crossroad Publishing Company, 1995), 228.

10. W. John Livesley, ed., *The DSM-IV Personality Disorders* (New York: Guilford Press, 1995), 265–66. Reprinted with permission from the *Diagnostic and Statistical Manual of Mental Disorders,* Third Edition. Copyright 1980 American Psychiatric Association.

11. Kennedy and Charles, 229, 235, 241.

12. W. Reich, *Character Analysis,* 3d ed (New York: Norton, 1956); cited in Beck and others, 310.

13. Beck and others, 46.

14. Ibid., 361.

15. Henry Cloud and John Townsend, *Safe People* (Grand Rapids, Mich.: Zondervan Publishing House, 1995), 28–29.

16. Ibid., 75–76.

17. H. S. Sullivan, *Clinical Studies in Psychiatry* (New York: Norton, 1956); cited in Beck and others, 310.

18. A. Angyal, *Neurosis and Treatment: A Holistic Theory* (New York: John Wiley & Sons, 1985); cited in Beck and others, 310.

19. V. F. Guidano and G. Liotti, *Cognitive Processes and Emotional Disorders* (New York: Guilford Press, 1983); cited in Beck and others, 314.

20. T. Millon and G. Everly, *Personality and Its Disorders* (New York: John Wiley & Sons, 1985); cited in Beck and others, 211.

21. Henry Cloud and John Townsend, *Boundaries: When to Say Yes, When to Say No to Take Control of Your Life* (Grand Rapids, Mich.: Zondervan Publishing House, 1992), 59.

22. Beck and others, 319, 321.

23. Kennedy and Charles, 238.

Chapter 2

1. John M. Oldham and Lois B. Morris, *The New Personality Self-Portrait* (New York: Bantam Books, 1995), 131, 133.

2. Theodore Millon, *Disorders of Personality, DSM III, Axis II* (New York: John Wiley and Sons, 1981), 142.

3. W. John Livesley, ed., *The DMV-IV Personality Disorders* (New York: Guilford Press, 1995), 178. Reprinted with permission from the *Diagnostic and Statistical Manual of Mental Disorders*, Third Edition. Copyright 1980 American Psychiatric Association.

4. Aaron T. Beck, Arthur Freeman, and Associates, *Cognitive Therapy of Personality Disorders* (New York: Guilford Press, 1990), 215.

5. Millon, 131.

6. Henry Cloud and John Townsend, *Boundaries: When to Say Yes, When to Say No to Take Control of Your Life* (Grand Rapids, Mich.: Zondervan Publishing House, 1992), 55, 59.

7. Beck and others, 362.

8. Eugene Kennedy and Sara C. Charles, M.D., *On Becoming a Counselor: A Basic Guide for Nonprofessional Counselors,* New Expanded Edition (New York: Crossroad Publishing Company, 1995), 243–45.

9. Beck and others, 216.

10. Henry Cloud and John Townsend, *Safe People* (Grand Rapids, Mich.: Zondervan Publishing House, 1995), 57.

11. Ibid., 37.

12. Millon, 150.

13. Beck and others, 216.

14. Millon, 152.

15. Ibid., 153.
16. Ibid., 156.

Chapter 3

1. John M. Oldham and Lois B. Morris, *The New Personality Self-Portrait* (New York: Bantam Books, 1995), 108–09.
2. F. C. Harrison, "Dependency—Responsibility—Morality: A Metapsychological Synthesis," *American Journal of Social Psychiatry* 7 (1987): 245–52; cited in Robert Bornstein, *The Dependent Personality* (New York: Guilford Press, 1993), 2.
3. Bornstein, 19.
4. Aaron T. Beck, Arthur Freeman, and Associates, *Cognitive Therapy of Personality Disorders* (New York: Guilford Press, 1990), 45.
5. Oldham and Morris, 128.
6. Beck and others, 289.
7. Theodore Millon, *Disorders of Personality, DSM III, Axis II* (New York: John Wiley and Sons, 1981), 112; Oldham and Morris, 128.
8. Ibid., 107.
9. Oldham and Morris, 128.
10. Ibid.
11. Beck and others, 44.
12. W. John Livesley, ed., *The DMV-IV Personality Disorders* (New York: Guilford Press, 1995), 241.Reprinted with permission from the *Diagnostic and Statistical Manual of Mental Disorders,* Third Edition. Copyright 1980 American Psychiatric Association.
13. Beck and others, 360.
14. Bornstein, 87.
15. Ibid., 88.
16. Oldham and Morris, 130.
17. Ibid.
18. Ibid.
19. Bornstein, 41.
20. Anne Wilson Schaef, *Co-dependency: Misunderstood and Mistreated* (New York: Harper and Row, 1986), 50.
21. Ibid., 39.
22. Charlotte Davis Kasl, *Many Roads, One Journey: Moving Beyond the Twelve Steps* (New York: HarperCollins, 1992), 8–9.
23. Oldham and Morris, 130.
24. Ibid.
25. Ibid.
26. Ibid.

Chapter 4

1. John M. Oldham and Lois B. Morris, *The New Personality Self-Portrait* (New York: Bantam Books, 1995), 87–88.
2. Otto Kernberg, *Severe Personality Disorders: Psychotherapeutic Strategies* (New Haven, Conn.: Yale University Press, 1984), 193.
3. Oldham and Morris, 99.
4. Theodore Millon, *Disorders of Personality, DSM-III, Axis II* (New York: John Wiley and Sons, 1981), 157, 169.
5. Ibid., 157.
6. Ibid., 167.
7. Ibid., 169.
8. W. John Livesley, ed., *The DMV-IV Personality Disorders* (New York: Guilford Press, 1995), 205. Reprinted with permission from the *Diagnostic and Statistical Manual of Mental Disorders,* Third Edition. Copyright 1980 American Psychiatric Association.
9. Aaron T. Beck, Arthur Freeman, and Associates, *Cognitive Therapy of Personality Disorders* (New York: Guilford Press, 1990), 361–62.
10. Ibid., 244.
11. Oldham and Morris, 101.
12. Beck and others, 235.
13. O. F. Kernberg, "Factors in the Treatment of Narcissistic Personality Disorder," *Journal of the American Psychoanalytic Association* 18 (1970): 51–58; cited in Millon, 175.
14. Beck and others, 235.
15. Millon, 163.
16. Ibid., 175.
17. Pia Mellody, *Facing Codependency* (San Francisco: Harper, 1989), 138; citing H. S. Sullivan, *Clinical Studies in Psychiatry* (New York: Norton, 1956).
18. Ibid.
19. Ibid.
20. Millon, 169.
21. Ibid., 179.
22. Ibid.
23. Eugene Kennedy and Sara C. Charles, M.D., *On Becoming a Counselor: A Basic Guide for Nonprofessional Counselors,* New Expanded Edition (New York: Crossroad Publishing Company, 1995), 299.
24. Ibid.
25. Beck and others, 256.
26. Millon, 177–178.
27. Beck and others, 248–49.

Chapter 5

1. John M. Oldham and Lois B. Morris, *The New Personality Self-Portrait* (New York: Bantam Books, 1995), 80–81.

2. Theodore Millon, *Disorders of Personality, DSM-III, Axis II* (New York: John Wiley & Sons, 1981), 61.

3. Ibid., 169.

4. D. L. Burnham, A. J. Gladstone, and R. W. Gibson, *Schizophrenia and the Need-Fear Dilemma* (New York: International Universities Press, 1969).

5. K. Horney, *Neurosis and Human Growth* (New York: Norton, 1950), 134.

6. W. John Livesley, ed., *The DSM-IV Personality Disorders* (New York: Guilford Press, 1995), 226. Reprinted with permission from the *Diagnostic and Statistical Manual of Mental Disorders,* Third Edition. Copyright 1980 American Psychiatric Association.

7. Aaron T. Beck, Arthur Freeman, and Associates, *Cognitive Therapy of Personality Disorders* (New York: Guilford Press, 1993), 359–60.

8. Ibid., 264.

9. L. Alden and R. Cappe, "A Comparison of Treatment Strategies for Clients Functionally Impaired by Extreme Shyness and Social Avoidance," *Journal of Consulting and Clinical Psychology* 54 (1986): 796–801.

10. J. Kagan, J. S. Reznick, and N. Snidman, "Biological Bases of Childhood Shyness," *Science* 240 (1988): 167–171.

11. Beck and others, 261.

12. S. A. Turner, D. C. Beidel, D. V. Dancu, and D. J. Keys, "Psychopathology of Social Phobia and Comparison to Avoidant Personality Disorder," *Journal of Abnormal Psychology* 95 (1986), 389–94.

13. T. J. Trull, T. A. Widiger, and A. Francis, "Covariation of Criteria Sets for Avoidant, Schizoid and Dependent Personality Disorders," *American Journal of Psychiatry* 144 (1987), 767–71.

14. Lynn Alden, "Short-term Structured for Avoidant Personality Disorder," *Journal of Counseling and Clinical Psychology,* 57:6 (1989), 756–64.

15. R. Alden and R. Cappe, "Interpersonal Process Training for Shy Clients," in *A Sourcebook on Shyness: Research and Treatment* (New York: Plenum Press, 1986), 343–56.

Chapter 6

1. John M. Oldham and Lois B. Morris, *The New Personality Self-Portrait* (New York: Bantam Books, 1995), 174.

2. Frank Koch, *Proceedings,* cited by Stephen R. Covey, *The 7 Habits of Highly Effective People* (New York: Fireside, 1989), 33.

3. Oldham and Morris, 157–58.

4. W. John Livesley, ed., *The DSM-IV Personality Disorders* (New York: Guilford Press, 1995), 49. Reprinted with permission from the *Diagnostic and Statistical Manual of Mental Disorders,* Third Edition. Copyright 1980 American Psychiatric Association.

5. Josephus, *Antiquities,* 15.26–76.

6. Ibid., 291.

7. Ibid., 295.

8. Ibid., 17.167; Josephus, *War,* 1.655.

9. D. Shapiro, *Neurotic Styles* (New York: Basic Books, 1965); F. M. Colby, W. S. Faught, and R. C. Parkinson, "Cognitive Therapy of Paranoid Conditions: Heuristic Suggestions Based on a Computer Simulation Model," *Cognitive Therapy Research* 3 (1979): 5–60.

10. See Shapiro, *Neurotic Styles,* 101.

11. So e.g., J. L. Pretzer, "Paranoid Personality Disorder: A Cognitive View" (paper presented at the annual meeting of the Association for Advancement of Behavior Therapy, Houston, Tex., 1985).

12. Livesley, 59.

13. Ibid., 46, 52.

14. Theodore Millon, *Disorders of Personality, DMS III, Axis II* (New York: John Wiley and Sons, 1981), 61.

15. Livesley, 47.

16. C. Marvin Pate and Calvin B. Haines, *Doomsday Delusions: What's Wrong with Predictions About the End of the World* (Downers Grove, Ill.: InterVarsity, 1995), 16–17.

17. D. S. Russell, *Apocalyptic Ancient and Modern* (Philadelphia, Penn.: Fortress, 1978), 64.

18. For example, see *Dignostic and Statistical Manual of Mental Disorders* (American Psychiatric Association: Washington, D.C., 1987), 338; I. D. Turkat and D. S. Banks, "Paranoid Personality and Its Disorder," *Journal of Psycopathology and Behavioral Assessment* 9 (1987), 295–304.

19. Aaron T. Beck, Arthur Freeman, and Associates, *Cognitive Therapy of Personality Disorders* (New York: Guilford Press, 1993), 108.

20. Pate and Haines, chapter 5.

21. Chris Fabry, *Spiritually Correct Bedtime Stories* (Downers Grove, Ill.: InterVarsity Press, 1995), 23–29.

Chapter 7

1. John M. Oldham and Lois B. Morris, *The New Personality Self-Portrait* (New York: Bantam Books, 1995), 227.

2. Ibid., 227–28.

3. Ibid., 243–45.

4. W. John Livesley, ed., *The DSM-IV Personality Disorders* (New York: Guilford Press, 1995), 120. Reprinted with permission from the *Diagnostic and Statistical Manual of Mental Disorders,* Third Edition. Copyright 1980 American Psychiatric Association.

5. Oldham and Morris, 246.

6. Ibid., 246–47.

7. Aaron T. Beck, Arthur Freeman, and Associates, *Cognitive Therapy of Personality Disorders* (New York: Guilford Press, 1993), 154.

8. Ibid.

9. Kenneth Barker, ed., *The NIV Study Bible* (Grand Rapids: Zondervan, 1985), 12.

10. Oldham and Morris, 248.

11. Ibid., 247, 249.

12. Ibid., 249.

13. Beck and others, 159.

14. Charles Colson, *America's Prison Crisis: The Problem/the Solution* (Washington, D. C.: Prison Fellowship Ministries, 1987), 29–30.

15. Ibid., 33–34.

16. Ibid., 50.

17. Ibid.

Chapter 8

1. John M. Oldham and Lois B. Morris, *The New Personality Self-Portrait* (New York: Bantam Books, 1995), 293–94.

2. Ibid., 307–08.

3. Aaron T. Beck, Arthur Freeman, and Associates, *Cognitive Therapy of Personality Disorders* (New York: Guilford Press, 1990), 201.

4. W. John Livesley, ed., *The DSM-IV Personality Disorders* (New York: Guilford Press, 1995), 148. Reprinted with permission from the *Diagnostic and Statistical Manual of Mental Disorders,* Third Edition. Copyright 1980 American Psychiatric Association.

5. Cited in Beck and others, 187.

6. Beck and others, 178.

7. Ibid., 181.

8. Oldham and Morris, 314.

9. Ibid., 315–16.

10. Ibid., 316.

11. J. Young, "Schema-focused Cognitive Therapy for Personality Disorders" (Center For Cognitive Therapy New York, 1987); cited by Oldham and Morris, 317.

Chapter 9

1. Stephen Covey, *The 7 Habits of Highly Effective People* (New York: Simon & Schuster, 1990), 128–29.